BENCH JOCKEY

Stories About The Milwaukee Brewers

It's my job to give viewers facts about how a team performed; the guy that got a base hit in the bottom of the ninth to win the game. It's important to the sports fan. 'Bench Jockey' brings to light things about the game of baseball you may have never seen, and in one instance in particular, never been aware of. Jim Cryns offers his collection of stories that touch the heart and reach out to the human experience inside and outside the batter's box.

-Len Kasper - Chicago Cubs

Jim Cryns goes where most storytellers don't. His insatiable curiosity about not just the 'what' but the 'why' make him unique. Jim's ability to reach into his vast archives of experiences, culled from decades of always asking the provocative questions, make anything he touches special. Box scores tell you facts. Bench Jockey tells you the stories behind the scores. If you are a true fan, you'll love it!

-Tim Van Vooren - Fox 6 Sports

BENCH JOCKEY INCLUDES STORIES ABOUT:

CC SABATHIA, PRINCE FIELDER, RYAN BRAUN, YOVANI GALLARDO, BEN SHEETS, COREY HART, JONATHAN LUCROY, ARAMIS RAMIREZ, TREVOR HOFFMAN, CRAIG COUNSELL, JOHN AXFORD, RANDY WOLF, LATROY HAWKINS AND MORE.

All articles included in this compilation were published in Brewers Gameday Magazine.

Each story is representative of the time it was published, including statistics.

For Kris, Zoe and Rory

Thanks to Len Kasper for saving my life at County Stadium. Or at the very least, preventing me from becoming a drooling vegetable. Thanks to Mario Ziino and Gregg Hoffmann.

BENCH JOCKEY

A PLAYER, COACH OR MANAGER WITH
THE TALENT OF ANNOYING AND
DISTRACTING OPPOSITION PLAYERS
AND UMPIRES FROM HIS TEAM'S
DUGOUT WITH VERBAL REPARTEE. THE
ART OF RIDING OPPOSITION PLAYERS
ENOUGH TO UNNERVE THEM (BUT NOT
ENOUGH TO ENRAGE THEM AND
PROVOKE A FIGHT) IS BELIEVED TO BE
FAST-FADING IN THE 21ST CENTURY
GAME.

BENCH JOCKEY

PRINCE FIELDER

Prince Fielder made it clear at the start of Spring Training this year that he wanted to concentrate on this season and not his possible free agency.

"I'm fully committed to the Brewers this season and won't focus on free agency until after the season," said the Brewers' MVP All-Star and candidate for the National League's Player of the Year honor.

True to his word, Fielder stayed on track in 2011. He didn't let any distraction cloud his mission to help lead the Brewers to their first National League Central Division crown.

"Right now, I play for the Brewers, and that would be selfish of me to think about next year, because I'm signed here, and I have a job to do here," Fielder told the Chicago Sun Times in another interview.

Nobody – his teammates, manager, coaches, front office, fans – can say Prince hasn't done his job, and then some.

The 27-year-old Fielder was having an MVP-type season, becoming the first player in the big leagues to reach and surpass 100 RBIs for the season – the fourth time he's crossed the century mark in his young career. In addition, Fielder topped the 30-homer mark for the fifth time, becoming the first Brewers player to ever accomplish that feat.

"When you're focused on winning, and your team is winning, the personal achievements will come," Fielder said. "If you're not winning, it's that much harder. This year, I wanted to go in with the focus of winning because we have the best team I've been on so far."

This season, Fielder has been a more complete hitter than ever before. He has hit to left field when necessary, breaking more than one shift opponents often put on him. He has been very patient at the plate, something he took big strides in doing in 2010. He has hit in the clutch better than ever.

But, his prodigious homers still are what people often want to talk about the most. They earned him the honor of serving as captain of the National League in the annual Home Run Derby during the All-Star Week in Phoenix back in July.

He didn't win that competition, but he did earn the All-Star Game Ted Williams Award, as well as Midsummer Classic MVP honor following his homer that put his team in the lead. The National League won the game 5-1.

"I love watching the highlights," Fielder admitted. "I don't want to show up the pitcher on the field, but I couldn't wait to see where the ball landed. I tried to take a quick look when I started my jog, but most of the time you never know where it hits until you see the highlights."

Fielder's been watching plenty of highlights this year, especially since the All-Star break. He has led the Brewers on a phenomenal journey through the Central Division standings. In August, the Brewers zoomed to the top thanks to a 25-5 run.

"You have to keep positive thoughts throughout the season, and watching highlights of your own home runs will definitely put you in a positive mood."

Fielder has always had power, even when he was tagging along with his father, Cecil, from big league park to big league park.

Once, when a former player was talking about a home run into the upper deck at Tiger Stadium, Prince said in a matter of fact manner, "yeah, I did that when I was 12."

"I'm big," Fielder told an MLB.com interviewer who asked about his power during the season. "I just always thought it was something I was supposed to have."

His power has drawn the admiration of another Brewers' power hitter, Ryan Braun.

"A lot of guys are big, but he's really explosive, too," Braun said. "When you see him swing the bat, it's like he has a toothpick in his hands. I think he could hold his own in the world's strongest man competition."

Braun and Fielder have been compared to the Milwaukee Braves' power tandem of Henry Aaron and Eddie Mathews, both Hall of Famers. They have formed a special chemistry and mutual admiration society, while also knowing they are different types of hitters.

"Braunie thinks up there more than I do," Fielder said. "I'm just going up there trying to hit it." Fielder has known the spotlight since he was signed in 2002. At each level of the minors, Fielder showed great power.

Once he made it to the Brewers, he again produced. He became the youngest player in baseball history to reach 50 homers, reaching the milestone back in 2007. Later in the season, Fielder was asked for the umpteenth time about possible upcoming free agency. This time, he did give what would be an ideal scenario in an MLB.com interview.

"I know this is a business and you have to look at it that way," he said. "But, if we could win the World Series, and I could stay here, it would be cool, too.

"Now that we're winning, I'm having fun."

RYAN BRAUN

In five big league seasons, Ryan Braun has made a name for himself. Braun hit a personal-best 23 straight games sandwiched around the All-Star Game – accomplishing the feat despite an injury that forced him out of action for eight games leading into the break.

That is what made his streak remarkable. In his first game back following the Midsummer Classic, Braun rapped out a double in his very first plate appearance – swinging the bat as if he hadn't missed a single game.

Though the 27-year-old outfielder had to skip the All-Star Game, he was truly honored to be named to the squad for the fourth time, and was scheduled to start his third straight Midsummer Classic. It was a small sacrifice to pay for the hitting star of the Brewers who led the Club to the playoffs for the second time in four seasons.

"I think it's special every time," Braun said of the honor. "I don't think I'll ever take it for granted. I have always taken pride in my work ethic, and to be selected, more or less confirms that you are working hard and playing well. It tells you that work is paying off."

By the end of August, Braun's hard work helped him climbed into the National League batting title race. No Brewers player ever won a batting champion. But the true incentive is what follows during the second half of the season – a trip to the postseason – which is everyone's focus when a team, like the Brewers, is in a position to contend for a pennant.

"I consider it motivating," he added. "You have

set a standard. I take pride in that and want to continue to work to achieve that level."

Braun had a great first half in many ways. Not only was he among the league leaders in average, home runs, RBI and runs most of the year, but he also signed an almost unprecedented long term contract early in the season. It will make him a Brewer until 2020, with an option for 2021.

"I wanted to do it for a lot of reasons," said Braun, who approached the ball club about the extension. "For one thing, it allows me to concentrate on baseball and winning for the next number of years."

Another feather in his cap came in September when he closed in on a milestone held by only one other Brewers player. He became only the second to ever hit at least 30 home runs and steal at least 30 bases in a season, joining Tommy Harper, who was a 30/30 player in 1970.

Braun could now join Robin Yount and Rollie Fingers as the only Brewers to earn league MVP honors. Together with teammate Prince Fielder, Braun is a legitimate candidate for the NL's top award.

"I'm proud to be a Milwaukee Brewer, I really am, and I'm proud to say that I'm going to continue to be a Milwaukee Brewer for at least the next 10 years," Braun shared. "It's something that's incredible for me.

"To be in one of the smallest markets in baseball and be able to have 3 million people come see us play every year, it's incredible. It's special to me. It's special to all of us and it makes it easy for me to want to stay here and to want to be a part of this organization going forward for the rest of my career."

Braun also cited players like Yount and Jim Gantner, who played their whole careers in Milwaukee.

"That's something that was a huge factor in me making the decision to stay here," Braun said. "You don't see that happen too often in sports anymore -- especially baseball. Doug Melvin mentioned Derek Jeter, Chipper Jones. Mariano Rivera.

"There really aren't many guys who have spent their whole career with one team. Obviously Robin was incredible and spent his entire career here. Tony Gwynn spent his entire career in San Diego, Cal Ripken in Baltimore. Those are all guys that I've admired."

Braun also admires his teammates with the current team and thinks the Brewers are poised to do some great things.

"I've been a part of a group of guys that have come in and tried to change the culture and get back to having the perception of being a winning organization," he said.

"Guys like Robin Yount played here, Gorman Thomas, Paul Molitor, and Jim Gantner. When all those guys were here it was a special place to play. I think the group of guys that we have here today -- not only the players, but the coaches -- have us heading in the right direction, getting back to being a team that other guys want to play for, being an attractive place for free agents."

Braun worked hard over the offseason and put on about 5-7 pounds, primarily in his legs, to increase his power.

"I don't want to add weight in my upper body," Braun said.

"I obviously am not the biggest guy (6-1, 210), at least among home run hitters. I have to do it with my legs and explosiveness. I want to stay flexible in my upper body."

That's typical of the professional, business-like way Braun goes about the game. He can be quite analytical about the physical and mental parts of the game, even the business side of the game.

"I enjoy doing what I can do to make the most of the ability I've been given," Braun said. "That means working hard to develop my skills and aptitude. I believe it also means learning about the overall game and industry beyond what goes on the field.

"For example, I think our facility here is probably as good as anywhere in baseball. Our locker room is incredible, our weight room is phenomenal. Our staff here, they take pride in everything they do, and that all goes a long way. That side of an organization is very important for a winning culture.

"We're really starting to be looked at as an organization that's committed to winning. And I think that's the biggest thing that's attractive to free agents, going somewhere where the team is going to be committed to winning, where ownership puts money back into the team and into the players and is committed to keeping the good players around."

Braun also has become part of the Milwaukee area business world, as a partner in two restaurants. He also has his own line of bats, clothing and fusion drink.

"I've been learning a lot," Braun said. "I was a business major at Miami and would like to be known for accomplishments in addition to baseball. I enjoy using my aptitude in that area.

"That doesn't mean putting down this game in any way. It's tremendously challenging. You have to respect the game to be able to play it." The way Braun plays it is how champions play it.

YOVANI GALLARDO

When the Brewers picked up right-handers Zack Greinke and Shaun Marcum last winter, some people asked, "who would be the ace of the starting rotation?"

Yovani Gallardo didn't really care about that question, but also has made the case that the designation should still be his.

"It doesn't really matter to me, or I think to anybody here," Gallardo said when asked the ace question in the spring. "We've added depth to our rotation. That's a good thing. It should give us a better chance to win."

Gallardo was the hottest pitcher in the National League at one point in the first half of the season, winning six straight decisions to post a 10-5 mark by the All-Star break.

After struggling to a 6.23 ERA in April, Gallardo was 5-1, with a 2.25 ERA and 1.13 WHIP in May. He won five straight, posting the fifth win with eight shutout innings in a 6-0 win over the Giants. He allowed only four hits in that game.

On May 7, Gallardo allowed only one hit in eight shutout innings against the Cardinals. The Cards didn't get that hit until the 8th when Daniel Descalso led off the inning with a single.

Gallardo took two losses and had a no-decision during the first three weeks in June, but bounced back for his ninth win in a decision over the Twins on June 26.

"What I've tried to do is fix what didn't go right in the previous start in the next start," Gallardo said after his win over Minnesota. "I try to keep improving each start. For me, command is everything.

"My rhythm was a little too quick in the early innings. That's happened a few times this season. I slowed it down and that allows me to get into more of a groove and have better command."

Gallardo says the key is to locating his fast ball. If he does that well, his breaking stuff can be more effective. Some, including his manager, would like to see him use a change-up more often.

"He has three great pitches with the curveball, the slider/cutter and fastball," Manager Ron Roenicke said. "If he can add that change-up in there, that's a lot of weapons because they're all plus pitches. With that stuff, you don't want him to work so hard. He should have some easy innings."

Gallardo was picked the Brewers' Most Valuable Pitcher last year for the second straight season. He went 14-7, with a 3.84 ERA, despite spending some time on the disabled list with a left oblique strain.

A key in 2010 was an adjustment, moving from the third base to first base side of the rubber.

"I think it's made it easier to throw strikes," Gallardo said at the time. "Coach (Rick) Peterson talks about creating lanes in the strike zone, and I think throwing from that side of the rubber has made it easier to get pitches into the lane."

Gallardo has continued to work on some adjustments with current pitching coach Rick Kranitz. "He's been great to work with," Gallardo said of Kranitz.

In 2010, Gallardo also signed a contract extension through 2014, with an option for 2015.

"They (the Brewers) drafted me, and I came up through their organization," Gallardo said. "I think we've built a good core here and can get better over time. This gives me a chance to develop along with the team."

Gallardo, who won a Silver Slugger Award at his position last season, led all big league pitchers with four homers and 10 RBI, while hitting .254. He has continued to hit well this season.

"Obviously, every starter wants to go out there and help themselves," Gallardo said. "I like hitting actually. I work on that part of my game."

Gallardo, a native of Fort Worth, Texas, was selected in the second round of the 2004 draft. He was projected early as the eventual ace of the Brewers' staff and made steady progress through the Minor League system.

The Brewers called him up in 2007 after he went 8-3 at AAA in Nashville. He went 9-5, with a 3.67 ERA, with the Brewers that year.

One of his major disappointments is that he could not be more a part of the 2008 Wild, Card playoff season. He had two stints on the disabled list, with injuries to both knees. He did return late in the season and made two appearances, including one start, against the Phillies in Division Series playoffs.

Now, Gallardo is poised to lead the Brewers in the playoffs. It doesn't matter whether he is referred to as the ace of the staff or not.

"I think everybody on this team is focused on winning," he said. "We know we have a talented, deep team that can go places."

CC SABATHIA

Carsten Charles Sabathia, better known as CC, knows exactly why the Brewers brought him to Milwaukee.

They wanted to get to the postseason for the first time since 1982. It worked.

Sabathia has been in complete control since the Brewers acquired him from the Cleveland Indians July 7 for four players – outfielder Matt LaPorta, the Brewers' top draft pick last year, pitchers Zack Jackson and Rob Bryson and a player to be named later.

Not only did he race to a 9-0 record in his first 10 starts, he did it convincingly. Sabathia registered six complete games, including three shutouts, striking out 85 batters in his first 88 innings of work.

In addition, Sabathia became only the third starting pitcher over the last 90 years to win his first nine decisions following a mid-season trade. He closed out August with a career best one-hitter against the Pittsburgh Pirates, earning his second straight National League Pitcher of the Month honor.

"I wanted to fit in and be another addition to a great team and get us to a championship," the 2007 American League Cy Young Award winner said. "I guess it says we have a great team."

Even Brewers General Manager Doug Melvin couldn't expect that type of production when he pulled out all the stops in landing the big lefthander.

Nonetheless, Melvin had to do it. But to do so, he had to trade the club's top prospect, along with promising talent, for the right to hope for the best.

"To bring in a player of CC Sabathia's ability was very encouraging for this organization," Melvin said. "It's one of the biggest trades for me in 13 years. It's a trade to take this ball club (to the next level)."

At the time of the trade, Melvin proclaimed, "We're going for it."

They certainly did.

"It was a huge boost to the fans, which have had a long drought here and maybe they thought this kind of thing could never happen," Melvin added. We just felt we needed to go for it."

Brewers' fans quickly embraced their new workhorse on the mound. It was an electric feeling at One Brewers Way when Sabathia made his National League debut a day after the trade was announced. Attendance figures for the game, projected to be in the low-30s, spiked to a sellout level of 42,533 nearly overnight. From that point on, the Brewers played before packed houses at Miller park right into September.

Each time Sabathia took the mound, fans greeted him with chants, "let's go, CC" while holding up signs that read: "CC you in the playoffs."

"The fans brought so much energy to the ballpark," Sabathia said. "This has been unbelievable. It has exceeded anything I would imagine the way I've been received here. This has been so much fun."

Fans may remember when Sabathia pitched at Miller Park in 2007. He took the mound for the Indians when the American League club had to move some early-April home games to Milwaukee because of a major snowstorm in Cleveland.

"I remember the slow motion wave," Sabathia said about that game. "I know this is a great city to play in. The fans are awesome. I'm not going to say I'm not going to be excited, because I am, but I know I have a job to do. Just go out and compete, stay under control.

"I just tried to fit in and do my job," he said. "Baseball's hard enough to play without added pressure. That's something that I don't think about or worry about."

Sabathia does seem to have fit in rather quickly. He already knew pitcher David Riske from their days in the Indians farm system, and Russell Branyan was a teammate in Cleveland. He and Ben Sheets talked a lot during the first game Sabathia spent on the Brewers' bench.

"We got a Cy Young Award pitcher who we could put at the top of our rotation along with Ben Sheets to give us one of the better pitching staffs we've had here," Melvin said.

Sabathia, who is 6-7, 290, also hit it off with Prince Fielder, another burly guy, right away. "When I first walked in, he asked me if I needed to borrow some (uniform) pants," Sabathia said. "He's probably the only guy with a pair I'd fit in."

There are no guarantees Sabathia's stay with the Brewers will go beyond this season. The Brewers and Sabathia know that. He turned down a four-year, $72 million contract extension offer from the Indians. At 28, and with his experience, he'll be a hot commodity on the open market over winter.

But, Melvin and Owner Mark Attanasio emphasized that Sabathia's acquisition showed how far the organization had come by looking at the turnstiles and the financial bottom line, as well as on the field. "The acquisition of CC was a credit to all of the fan support that this organization has enjoyed over the last few years," said Melvin. "Without their support, we would not be in a position to acquire a pitcher of this caliber."

Attanasio added, "I was in the fortunate position to say 'okay' (to the deal). It was my privilege to do that. We've always tried to adopt a buyer's mindset. Top to bottom, this organization is focused on winning."

And with Sabathia slotted in the Brewers rotation that already featured Sheets, Manny Parra, Dave Bush and Jeff Suppan, winning became contagious.

BEN SHEETS

Ben Sheets has tried not to look back or forward this season.

The Brewers' All-Star pitcher has stayed focused on the present, and the task of winning baseball games.

Other than a mid-season hiccup and a forearm injury in mid-September, Sheets is and will continue to keep dealing on the mound. He has been locked in, posting a career high in victories while setting a personal best of 20 consecutive scoreless innings over three starts in August when the Brewers posted a 20-7 mark.

Earlier in the year, he missed one start because of some tenderness in his shoulder area, before experiencing some tightness in his throwing arm down the stretch. But he's worked through the rough patch, steering the Brewers to their first postseason action in 26 years.

From Spring Training on, the 30-year-old right-hander said he would concentrate on pitching, and not his contract status. Sheets is eligible for free agency after this season.

"To me, that's business and that's totally different than baseball," Sheets said. "I've never worried about it, and I'm not going to worry about it. That has no bearing on how I play the game. I can honestly say that's never crossed my mind when I'm on the field, or even during the season. There's plenty of time between seasons for all of that to happen."

By winning 10 games in the first half, Sheets became the first Brewers pitcher selected to start the midsummer classic for the National League – his club-record fourth invitation to the All-Star game. He did not disappoint, pitching two scoreless innings with three strikeouts.

He said he was very excited about starting the game, but was able to calm himself down before the outing at Yankee Stadium.

"It's weird, because it became a baseball game once I got out there," Sheets said. "Even when I got in the dugout and the game started, everything just kind of calmed down, which was good."

Though the game went 15 innings, the American League prevailed at 4-3.

Right before the All-Star break, Sheets got some help at the top of the rotation when the Brewers traded for CC Sabathia. The two meshed almost immediately and have given the team a dynamite back-to-back combo from either side of the mound.

"It's been great," Sheets said of the addition of the former Cy Young Award winner. "We talk pitching a lot when we're not out there. It's good to have somebody like CC at the top of our rotation."

Sheets admitted it's been an up and down season. For a while, he was not going very deep into games. After a complete-game win at Atlanta on May 23 boosted Sheets' record to 9-1 and lowered his ERA to 2.59, he hit a wall, pitching six or fewer innings in all but two of his next five starts.

"The sky is not falling," Sheets said at the time. "If I could have won two or three of those games, nobody would think I'm in a rut. As a pitcher, though, your success depends on everything."

Sheets straightened himself out and started going deeper into games. In early August, Sabathia and

Sheets pitched back-to-back complete game shutouts against the Washington Nationals. That was the first time Brewers' pitchers had accomplished that feat since 1992, when Cal Eldred and Chris Bosio did it.

"I think 'complete game,' when I toe the slab," Sheets said. "I go for it from the beginning. Most times you fall short, but oh well."

The one time Sheets has looked back this season was during the Beijing Olympics in August. An Olympic hero in the 2000 Games in Sydney, Australia, Sheets was asked to look back a lot by media. He did so willingly and admitted, "I follow the Games with interest."

Of course, Brewers' fans looked at Sheets as the soon-to-be ace of the staff after the 2000 Olympics. Many still wonder what more he could have accomplished if he had been able to stay healthy throughout his time with the Brewers.

Sheets doesn't feel sorry for himself because of his past injuries. "I don't feel sorry for myself one bit," said Sheets. "It's the hand you're dealt. Nobody wants to get hurt."

He primarily has concentrated on helping the Brewers get into the playoffs, for the first time in his career.

"When you look back at the end of the year, you are who you are," Sheets said. "Your numbers are what they are. That's all it is.

"We have the best chance of getting into postseason since I've been here. That's what I'm concentrating on at this point. The other things will take care of themselves."

COREY HART

It's hard to miss Corey Hart. At 6-foot-6, he stands tall in any batting order. Fortunately, he fits in well in the Brewers lineup in more ways than one.

In 2008, the 26-year-old right fielder solidified his standing as a legitimate threat in the Milwaukee batting order by becoming the first Brewers player to hit more than 20 home runs and steal more than 20 bases in back-to-back seasons.

Nevertheless, the soft-spoken Hart would sooner fly under the radar.

"We have so many stars on this team." Hart said. "Braunie, Prince, they get the attention they deserve. I really prefer to remain low key, do what I can to produce and help the team any way I can."

That might be how Hart likes to operate, but it's been difficult for him to do so this season, particularly after Brewers fans made it known how they felt about him at mid-season.

Even his peers recognize his production. During a Final Vote campaign for the All-Star Game, the Brewers' players did short television spots urging fans to vote for Hart as the 32nd player on the National League squad.

Hart drew eight million votes and made it to the big game, playing the last several innings in right field. In fact, the Twins' Justin Morneau just beat Hart's strong throw to the plate for another AL win.

"The fans really responded. I got a ton of votes," Hart said. "It was hard not to take notice and stay low key. My teammates and fans were talking about it.

My wife was calling me to find out the latest. It was a lot of fun.

"Playing in the game was an incredible experience. That's something you'll never forget the rest of your life."

Hart said the whole season became a high profile happening when the Brewers made the postseason for the first time since 1982.

"You play so many games it's hard to get peaked for every one, but that's not a problem when we play (for something)," he said. "The fans get into it so much. You can't help but get into it as a player, too. It's a lot of fun."

The key was to stay focused even after going 20-7 in August and then slumping to open the final month of the season.

"It can be tough, but we still had the games to play," Hart said. "I think going through last season helped. We knew what it (would) take."

Hart said the key for him the last two years has been playing every day. That wasn't always the case. He started last season in a three-way platoon, but then moved to the forefront and played just about every day in right or center. He finished with a .295 average, 24 homers and 81 RBI in 140 games.

"Once I got that chance, I was able to adjust and settle into my game," he added. "I've been able to continue to do that this year."

On his way up through the minors, Hart played third base, first base and several outfield positions. He has settled into right field this season and loves it.

"I really do love playing right," he said. "I feel very comfortable out there. I think with Cam (Mike Cameron) in center and Braunie (Ryan Braun) in left, we have a solid outfield, with some speed and good arms."

An 11th round pick in the 2000 draft, Hart demonstrated he could hit early in his pro career. He hit .340 in rookie ball in 2001 and had 10 homers and 84 RBI in A ball in 2002.

He led the league while in AA ball with 149 hits, 40 doubles and 94 RBI at Huntsville in 2003. He hit .281 in 121 games at Triple A at Indianapolis and appeared in one game for the Brewers in 2004. Hart split his time between AAA and the Brewers in 2005-06 and then arrived to stay last season.

He's been with Fielder, J.J. Hardy, Rickie Weeks and some of the other young players now with the Brewers on his way up through the farm system. He hopes they can collectively take the next big step to a championship.

"Last year was a learning experience for us," he said. "Obviously, this is another whole level and none of us had been through it here before."

Now they have.

JONATHAN LUCROY

All season long, Jonathan Lucroy's name has been mentioned every time the topic of National League Most Valuable Player is discussed. And rightfully so. Just ask the Brewers General Manager.

"There's no doubt in my mind that Jonathan has shown he should be in the MVP talk," Doug Melvin said. "He's had a year like Ryan Braun had in his MVP season."

The Brewers' catcher has been the most consistent and productive among his peers and on defense, the five-year veteran has been stellar handling the Milwaukee pitching staff.

He became the first modern day catcher to lead the league in doubles (53) when he also became the third Brewers' player to top 50 doubles in a season. Among all the clutch hits, the record chasing doubles and big home runs Lucroy has had, one game stands out to Melvin as the catalyst of the Brewers postseason run.

"I think one game stands out to me," Melvin reflected. It brought this team together. We were in Arizona back in June. Ryan Braun was hit by a pitch to load the bases and Jonathan wasted little time greeting a new pitcher by hitting the first pitch for a grand slam homer.

"That doesn't happen too often. But in this instance, it was a statement that this team stood together and wasn't about to be intimidated. I truly believe the confidence flowed after that."

Perhaps that's why it was no surprise that Lucroy was elected and eventually started behind the plate for the National League at the All-Star Game in

Minneapolis one month later.

Again, he showed it with his performance in one of the more entertaining Midsummer Classics in recent memory by collecting a pair of run scoring doubles in his two at-bats. Lucroy helped the Nationals erased an early 3-0 deficit, though the American League eventually won the game, 5-3.

"It was an honor for me to be part of it," Lucroy said following his All-Star Game debut. "I got some good pitches to hit and I was able to capitalize on them."

Lucroy was the sixth Brewers' catcher named to an All-Star team – the first since David Nilsson in 1999 and the first to start the contest since Ted Simmons in 1983.

For the record, Lucroy got the nod after the Cardinals Yadier Molina injured his hand leading up to the All-Star Game.

"I felt bad about 'Yadi' getting hurt," Lucroy added after winding up the first half of the season with a sparkling .315 batting average, nine home runs and 44 RBI. "Getting a hand injury like that, I know what it feels like because I've had two of them. It's a tough situation."

But Lucroy deserved selection, and among some experts, he deserved a starting assignment. He spent much of the first half ranked in the top five in several hitting categories in the NL.

He continued to shine in the second half, ranking among the National League leaders in batting average, doubles, extra-base hits and hits. Lucroy is also very good behind the plate and may be the best in the game at framing pitchers. Which means, when a pitch and the glove meet, that's where the action should stop. The catcher should have enough strength to stop the momentum of the ball so that strikes don't turn into balls. Lucroy has perfected that technique.

Moreover, according to a Baseball Prospectus study conducted earlier this season, Lucroy has gained more than 40 runs by getting more than 280 extra strike calls since he burst on the scene in 2010. He gets extra strikes for his pitchers both on the bottom and outside edges of the strike zone.

"I watched video of myself from after I was drafted, my first year in the Minor Leagues, and it was terrible. It was embarrassing," Lucroy said. "Now, I take a lot of pride in getting those pitches for guys. It's hard enough for pitchers to throw strikes anyway. I try to do my best, not necessarily framing the ball, but giving the umpire a good look."

Lucroy has also gotten a good look since moving up in the batting order this season. "I batted third a lot in high school and lower levels, but when I got here you had players like Ryan Braun and Aramis Ramirez," he said. "I do feel comfortable in those spots. I like having an opportunity to drive in guys."

"I've always felt like I was a 'hitting guy' before I was a 'defense guy,' but when you get to the big leagues, you want to be an all-around player. That's what I'm trying to be."

Lucroy thinks he played better than ever in the first half because the team played so well. "It takes four wheels to move a car," he said. "If you only have one or two working, the machine doesn't work well. We've had all four wheels working and the machine has run well. It's easier to contribute when the guys around you are playing so well."

But in the second half, the Brewers had a couple of slumps, which tightened the Central Division race. Over the long haul, those things are going to happen, even to good teams.

"We had games where we pitched and didn't hit," Lucroy began. "We had games where we hit and didn't pitch. It's a long season and you got to find that middle ground. Keep things simple." Just like hitting.

"It's a game of failure for a reason," he added. You just got to deal with it, move on and keep on working. It's the only game in the world where you can get a hit three out of 10 times for 10 years and be in the Hall of Fame."

Lucroy has become more of a team spokesman and leader in recent years. He often is sought out by reporters after games and serves as the Kwik Trip spokesman for the Brewers.

"It's not something I seek out," he said. "I prefer to make my statements with my play on the field, but I try to be cooperative and will speak up when I think it's right."

It's easy to see how he has shined and has become a rising star.

"Basically, I got my chance because of injuries," said Lucroy, who was rushed to the big leagues in 2010 because of an injury to catcher Greg Zaun. "It was learning under fire. I was called up earlier than they had planned. As it stands, that first three quarters of a season, while tough at times, was a good learning experience."

In 2011, Lucroy signed a five-year contract extension. "I talked with Ryan (Braun) quite a bit after he signed his extension," Lucroy said. "It was great to put those things behind me long term and concentrate on baseball."

He improved to .265 with 12 home runs and 59 RBI in 2011. Though limited in 2012 due to injury, he hit a career best .320.

And last year, Lucroy was healthy and established. His numbers rose, leading the with 82 RBI, and batted .303 over his final 111 games to boost his batting average to .280 by season's end. This year, he's been the glue that has kept the Brewers pennant hopes intact. And to him, that's more important than any MVP talk.

"I don't let that stuff enter my mind," Lucroy said of the rumors. "All I want to do is win for my team and have a chance to put a ring on my finger." As for comparisons between this team and Milwaukee's last playoff team in 2011, Lucroy believes the Brewers, who have been in first place practically all year long in 2014 is better balanced.

"We're well rounded," he said. "I think we have better overall pitching than we had in 2011. Our defense is much better, too.

"We may not have the power we had then but man-for-man I think we're better balanced.

"I can tell you this, we came out and had fun (this year). We stayed relaxed and we didn't put any added pressure on ourselves. We came together and it showed our character."

ARAMIS RAMIREZ

Aramis Ramirez doesn't consider himself an "elder statesman" or "role model" for the younger Brewers, especially his fellow Dominicans Carlos Gomez, Jean Segura and Wily Peralta.

At 36, however, the veteran third baseman is looked to for leadership by the younger players, as well as for his production which has been his trademark throughout his 14 years in the big leagues.

Perhaps his best example of both came earlier this summer when he was voted to his third All-Star Game – his first as a Brewers player and his first since 2008. Making it even more noteworthy was the fact that Ramirez was selected as a starter for the National League at third base, again a first by a Brewers third baseman. In the process, he became the team's oldest to start in the Midsummer Classic and the oldest to collect a hit. Make it two hits and a run scored.

"That was an honor," Ramirez said. "I've been an All-Star before, but to be voted in by the fans was something special."

Fellow teammates Jonathan Lucroy and Gomez also earned starting assignments, while closer Francisco Rodriguez managed to pitch in the game. Lucroy collected a pair of run-scoring doubles, Gomez made a couple of catches in the outfield including a nice running grab, and Rodriguez tossed a scoreless frame.

"I think as a group we represented the team well," Ramirez said, despite the Nationals' 5-3 loss.Though he may not admit it, his teammates certainly admire the way he goes about his business, especially this season.

Ramirez was instrumental in the Brewers' pennant chase as a stabilizing presence in the lineup.

"He's been doing it for a long time," said Gomez. "You have to look up to him and learn from him." Yet, the modest Ramirez says, "I don't see myself that way. I just try to come here every day and do what I can to help my team win. I had some guys who really helped me when I first came up (with Pittsburgh in 1998) and showed me some of the differences between the big leagues and the minors.

"I will help them in that way. If they are doing something I think they shouldn't, I'll talk to them. I'm not a real vocal guy though. I'm not going to get on a guy's case. I like to lead by example."

That's what makes him well respected among his teammates.

"He's not looking for the spotlight," said Brewers General Manager Doug Melvin. "He has a quiet presence but the players take notice, especially the Latin ones.

"Aramis likes to come to the park, get in the batter's box and perform. He just loves to hit with men on base. And, when he's out of the lineup, we miss him."

He is definitely a leader on this team, not only with the Latin players, but with everyone. All our players watch him closely and see how he keeps everything under control. He never panics. He keeps working. That's what he brings to the ballclub.

Ramirez has been doing that, first with the Pirates, then the Cubs and now since 2011 with the Brewers. A lifetime .285 hitter, Ramirez ranks all-time among third basemen in home runs, doubles and runs batted in.

"I think I focus more when runners are in scoring position," Ramirez said. "Not press. There's a big difference. If you press, you won't get it done. You have to focus and not try to do too much. There are a lot of ways you can get runners in."

In 2012, he became only the second Brewers player to collect 50 or more doubles in a season – leading the National League in that category as well as extra base hits, joining Heinie Zimmermann (1912) and Sal Bando (1973) as the only third basemen to lead the league in both departments.

That same year, he came within a whisker of earning a Gold Glove on defense, posting a career best .977 fielding percentage. Ramirez committed only seven errors in 300 total chances.

"He has been pretty consistent throughout his career," Melvin observed. "With a couple of more years, he may be getting close to Hall of Fame numbers.

"He performs very well defensively. He has plus arm strength and very good hands, soft hands; he knows where to play hitters. He goes under the radar because he's sort of quiet but a great competitor."

Health has been Ramirez's main challenge through much of his career. He made 10 trips to the disabled list, including missing three weeks in May with a strained hamstring. And yet, he has remained productive.

"Staying healthy is very important," Ramirez said. "That's my top goal every season."

Ramirez played basketball and baseball as a kid in Santo Domingo, DR. He focused more on baseball after age 13 and signed with the Pirates as a non-drafted free agent in 1994.

It didn't take long for Ramirez to establish himself as a productive hitter. He was called up to the Pirates for the first time in 1998 and struggled in relatively short stints for a couple seasons.

In 2001, however, he hit .300 with 34 homers and 112 RBI. That was the start of two decent seasons with the Pirates. He then was traded in 2003 to the Cubs, along with Kenny Lofton, for Jose Hernandez, pitcher Matt Bruback and infielder Bobby Hill.

With the Cubs, Ramirez drove in 100 or more runs four times, made the All-Star team two times and appeared in three NLDS series and a NLCS series.

After a couple straight seasons that were marred by injuries in 2009-10, the Cubs decided to go another route at third, making Ramirez available as a free agent.

Melvin wasted little time signing the veteran to a three-year contract with a mutual option for 2015.

"Signing with the Brewers worked out very well for me," Ramirez said. "It was good for my family (wife, Yudith, and three children) because it was still in the same region of this country. It's been a good stay here and we have a chance to do some good things this year.

"We're pretty good," Ramirez said. "We have a good team." Ramirez is focused. And, while he has enjoyed the accolades of being one of the most consistent players in the game, one thing has eluded him.

"I've done everything from the All-Star Game to [winning a] Silver Slugger. I've done it all basically, but the one thing I'm missing is that ring and that's what I'm looking for."

"I work hard and take pride in what I do. I want to be good. I don't want to be considered a regular player. I want my teammates to count on me to get the job done."

Though he may not acknowledge it, in most circles that's called leading by example.

TREVOR HOFFMAN

AC/DC's "Hell's Bells" will likely become one of the favorite tunes at Miller Park this season.

When it's played, it signals the entrance of the Brewers new closer Trevor Hoffman, the big leagues' all-time saves leader with an amazing 554 in a 16-year Hall of Fame career.

"Well it fires me up and the crowd," Hoffman, 41, said when he signed as a free agent with the Brewers over the winter. "I hope the fans will enjoy it. Miller time and Trevor time sounds pretty good.

"It's part of the routine. It allows me to focus. It part of the theatrics of the game. But I know I have a job to do. I think everyone will have a good time with it."

While Hoffman identified by his own song and saves, he sort of graciously snuck up on his celebrity and success.

"I think it happened in part because a lot of people were sleeping already when I was doing my thing on the West Coast in San Diego," Hoffman said. "I was going my job after a lot of people had already gone to bed."

Hoffman also doesn't blow people away with a 100 mph fast ball when he's doing his thing. His out-pitch has been a great changeup for years.

"The changeup has been a big key," he said. "Most late innings guys have an out-pitch of some kind. Developing that changeup early in my career has made a big difference.

"But, I think even a bigger key has been the ability to throw strikes with my fast ball. If you can do that, and get ahead of the hitter right away, you can play off that with your out-pitch.

"What makes it effective is strike one, regardless of how you get it. It's easier to pitch when you're ahead in the count. It's important to throw strikes, it's important to pound the zone with a number of pitches. Regardless if the hitter knows what's coming, it's important to be in a pitcher's count and rely on your defense."

The Brewers made it very clear they wanted Hoffman as their closer. That pursuit was the key to the veteran choosing Milwaukee over the Dodgers.

"This was the right choice because of the people I was able to talk to," Hoffman said. "Mr. (Doug) Melvin reached out while on his vacation to communicate with me because he feels strongly about this ball club. Mr. (Ken) Macha gave me a call as well. Roger (Caplinger) the trainer was an important factor in my decision. I have some things that I'm used to doing. It was something that fit.

"I'm looking forward to setting down some roots here. I've heard some great things about the community. Mike Cameron told me a lot of good things about the organization that was valid."

Melvin was unabashed about the Brewers' pursuit of Hoffman. "We wanted to continue to build the momentum from last year's postseason and Trevor Hoffman will help us with that," Melvin said.

"We still have postseason and a championship in our minds. He'll definitely help us to go forward. Having someone like Trevor at the back end of our bullpen will be a plus for us."

Hoffman was originally signed by the Reds as an infielder in 1989. He spent two years in the minors before Jim Lett, his manager at Charleston and now a Brewers' coach at AA Huntsville, recommended he try pitching. Despite the fact he had never pitched at any level, including high school, he made the switch and had 12 saves and a 1.87 ERA his first season on the mound. As a reliever, he made it to the big leagues in 1993 and has been there ever since. Thirteen times he has recorded 30 or more saves in a season, including nine times topping 40 saves, and in 1998 – the same year Hells Bells became his calling card – he peaked at 53 saves.

The Brewers let Hoffman set his own pace in spring training. "I'm a big believer in preparation, physically and mentally," Hoffman said. "I appreciate them having the confidence that I will be ready."

However, early in camp, Hoffman strained his oblique muscle on the right side of his ribcage. At first it didn't seem serious. But over the next few weeks it didn't improve. He was official placed on the 15-day disabled list on March 30 and was expected to miss the first week or so of the regular season. It marked only the second time in his career he had opened a season on the DL.

The Brewers are not worried. Because of his conditioning regiment, and because he keeps himself in great shape, they don't expect this to nag him all season. "The workouts change with age," Hoffman said. "I have to listen to my body. I have to figure out what works and what doesn't."

One thing was apparent about Hoffman in camp. He quickly established himself as a good clubhouse guy. It's something he believes in.

"To get respect you have to give respect," he said. "I'm always looking for the good fit. Chemistry is

very important. You can't quantify it. It doesn't have a
stat. Everyone understands its value. Those are some of
the things you talk about in the clubhouse. Those are
the things I value. You cultivate it. You work at it.

"I'm excited to be here. There's momentum
here. There's a culture that is developing, and a player
like myself, who's been around a long time, I was
looking for an opportunity to be a part of something
like that. It's invigorating to be the new kid on the
block and to be part of something positive."

CRAIG COUNSELL

When you list Major Leaguers from Wisconsin, it reads like a leaflet of 'famous sports legends' from the movie Airplane. You've got Jimmy Gantner, Jerry Augustine, Bob Uecker and few others.

The cold, bony grip of age grasps us by the collar and delivers an impersonal yet vigorous shake. It's not all that pleasant. You begin to feel aches and pains you had only associated with your parents or grandparents. In your youth you laughed in the face of maturity. Then came that horrid day when you have a personal epiphany – hey, that's me. I'm a parent or grandparent.

Brewers Manager Craig Counsell is 46 years old. That's young for a manager, but a bit long in the tooth for a player. On the whole, Counsell seemed to defy the slings and arrows of aging. To him, growing older is a mindset, a subjective thing.

Counsell says keeping abreast of contemporary music helps him stave off the baggage of age.

"You've got to stay up with current music," he says from his perch in the dugout during a recent home-stand. "It's how you stay connected."

When Counsell strode to the plate as a player, the fans heard Jimmi Hendrix's 'All Along The Watchtower.' While familiar, you have to be of a certain age to even know who Hendrix was to the music scene. When Counsell played, most teammates were born long after Hendrix moved on to the purple haze.

"I think the guys can relate to Hendrix, he's kind of lasted," Counsell added. "We play some other Hendrix songs on the plane."

Counsell says he listens to the stuff younger players do, but doesn't necessarily inhale.

"It's not my favorite music but I listen to it, and I enjoy it," he says. "We listen to Rick Ross and it's fun because everybody likes him and I like listening to it. Music is a bit part of what bonds people, for sure."

If music has played even a small part in this season's team chemistry and success, then the clubhouse attendant should turn the volume up to eleven. When you talk with Counsell, you realize he's a guy who has been around the block, and there's that unspoken aura about him. He's not necessarily sagacious, but he thinks before he speaks, a rare quality in the light-speed world of texting and tweeting inane ramblings.

Watching Counsell at the plate, you can almost hear his mind churning. He's arguably one of the best players in clutch situations. He's not going to swing at too many pitches out of the zone and Counsell is going to make the pitchers earn their keep. Counsell gets on base largely by walking, and that's fine with him. He raises pitch counts, fouls off a lot of pitches and is as stingy with his swings as a widow on a pension.

"We get all this information on pitchers, then you've got the stuff you're doing with your own swing to get better," Counsell says. "Then you run that all through your head and hopefully make a good swing."

Similar to the legendary Ted Williams, more times than not Counsell is going to swing at a strike.

"For me, plate discipline has been an important part," he offered. "If you don't have power, you've just got to get on base. That's the way I've always thought about it."

Counsell is the proverbial local boy made good. He went to Whitefish Bay High School and later Notre Dame University, the same school his father attended. His father, John Counsell, worked in the community relations department for the Brewers while Craig was growing up, so Craig had a front row seat to the inner workings of baseball. Though he never discussed it with Craig, John, who played in the Minnesota Twins organization, knew that his son had a gift.

Craig had the ears of two future Hall of Famers in Robin Yount and Paul Molitor. With that dynamic duo, he observed unwavering dedication, determination and desire, hallmarks for baseball longevity and productivity. Craig got to know these guys off the field too, and noticed they were the same guys no matter where they were—and that resonated with him.

"I spent a lot of time in the clubhouse and on the field at County Stadium," Counsell says. "That stuff wears off on you. It's like a kid whose dad is an auto mechanic. He knows how to fix cars better than the other kids, it's not that much different."

If you had watched Counsell in high school, you would have noticed he was head and shoulders above the other players. However, by his own admission he wasn't bigger or more physical than any of the other players.

"If there was something that stood out, I think I knew the game better," he says. "I just spent more time around baseball than most kids, so I just had a better feel for the game than most people."

The hallmarks of Counsell's career are his two World Series rings. Most players would gnaw off an arm for just one of those hunks of jewels.

In 1997, he earned a championship with the Marlins and in 2001, he rejoiced with the Diamondbacks, taking home MVP honors during the National League Championship Series.

He says there's no doubt playing in his hometown is special.

"I decided to come back here to play," Counsell says. "It was mostly my decision to do it and I could have played at other places. I wanted to play here because the Brewers were important to me."

Counsell says he wanted to be part of the teams that made baseball important in the state. "Whatever happens, going forward, I think that's been a success for sure," he says. He was honored at Miller Park with a bobble-head promotion.

During his first trip to the plate, the crowd stood and applauded for what seemed like ten minutes. Brewers announcer Brian Anderson called it a 'goose bump' moment.

"To paraphrase Jerry Maguire, Counsell completes this team," Anderson says.

As the sold-out crowd let Counsell know how much he meant to them, he characteristically kept his head down. He was deeply touched by the gesture.

His last year as a player was forgettable and he knew it. The fans still treated him as a treasured part of the team's history.

"I think it just shows you've made a connection with fans. In a lot of places I'd be booed out of the stadium. I'm totally aware. I think they fans feel like they know you well enough to kind of know what you're going through, and appreciate what you're going through."

JOHN AXFORD

John Axford no longer needs to stand in future Hall-of-Famer Trevor Hoffman's shadow. In 2011, 'The Axman,' as he is referred as, stood in the bright lights of his own fame, leading the Brewers to the National League Central Division crown.

Axford established himself as one of Major League Baseball's top closers this season by establishing a new Brewers record with 46 saves, becoming only the second Brewers pitcher to register 40 or more saves in a season.

"I still get a lot of questions about Trevor, which is fine," said Axford, who earned 24 saves in 2010 when he replaced Hoffman, who faltered early in the season. "He was one of the greats, and handled everything last season with a great deal of class.

"It could have been awkward, but he made sure it wasn't. He helped me a great deal, and to watch how hard he worked to get himself back on track, even near the end of his career, showed a great deal about his character and makeup."

Axford admitted that his situation this season is a lot different.

"Last year, in Spring Training, I was just trying to make the team," Axford said. "I fell short and then when Trevor struggled, I came up in May."

In addition to his 24 saves, Axford won eight of 10 decisions, struck out nearly three times as many batters as he walked and finished with a 2.48 ERA.

"It really came together," he said. "For me, the key is throwing strikes. I was a starter early in my career and didn't have a lot of time in relief. It is a little different, especially in the closer role.

This season, the job was his. And though he blew two of his first five save opportunities, he never altered his approach.

"You have to come out throwing strikes early," Axford added. "You can't afford to get behind in the count. You have to go right after hitters."

He didn't let the April struggles get to him. By May, he was swinging a mighty axe.

"It was pretty tough for a day or two, but I came out of it feeling much better," he said.

New Brewers Manager Ron Roenicke didn't panic when Axford labored as the closer in early-April. He had missed a couple of the early Spring Training workouts at Maryvale due to food poisoning, which put him behind in camp.

"His command was off during the spring and I know he wanted to get off to a good start this year," Roenicke said. "I knew once he got a couple of clean innings he would have the confidence that he had last year."

Axford is a native of Canada and still lives there. Despite the weather, he continued to work hard in the off-season, following a workout routine that was established in part at "Camp Hoffman" last year.

He and his wife, who bought a home in Hamilton, Ontario, Canada, worked out in a trainer's garage, even in the dead of winter. "I learned how important it is to be in shape," said the 6-5 Axford. "It was cold, but we worked up a sweat."

Axford was drafted in 2001 by Seattle, but chose to go to Notre Dame, where he pitched as a freshman in the College World Series. He underwent Tommy John surgery on his right elbow in 2004 and managed only three innings for the Irish in 2005.

The Reds nevertheless chose him in the 2005 draft, but he chose to attend Canisius College for the 2006 season.

Axford, who turned 28 this season, pitched in an independent league and worked as a bartender for awhile. He had just about given up on making it to the big leagues when he hooked on with the Brewers.

In 2009, Axford ascended from Class A Brevard County of the Florida State League to the Majors in one season. He went 9-1 with a 2.77 ERA in 45 relief appearances for Brevard County, Class AA Huntsville of the Southern League and Class AAA Nashville of the Pacific Coast League. He struck out 89 batters in 68.1 innings.

The Brewers brought him up on Sept. 7 of 2009, and he appeared in seven games, recording a 3.52 ERA while holding opponents to a .179 average. He recorded his first big league save on the final day of the season, as he preserved a 9-7, 10-inning victory at St. Louis for Hoffman. Of course, he would come to Hoffman's relief again in 2010.

His Cinderella story on his path to the Majors, along with his Rollie Fingers-like mustache and a trivia contest that he hosts on Twitter, have made him a cult hero among Milwaukee fans.

"All closers seem to have something, whether it's a song like Trevor had or something else," he said. "My mustache is sort of my thing, especially in Milwaukee where Rollie pitched. My background getting to the big leagues also kind of fits the town and fans.

"It's fun for the fans, which is good because we have great fans. Ultimately, though, you have to go out there and get people out. If you do that, you'll likely be a fan favorite and are doing your job."

RANDY WOLF

He was born in Canoga Park, California, shortly before his cinematic hero Darth Vader took to the screen. If you're too young to remember, Vader was to the galaxy what Prince Fielder was to opposing pitchers.

Wolf admits he owns a lot of memorabilia from the Star Wars franchise. If he has the bed sheet and pillowcase combo replete with all the characters, he hasn't mentioned it. But devotion has its limits. Wolf says he's not a fan of the second trilogy.

"Of course not," Wolf says. "They changed Yoda's face, and I won't even go near Jar Jar Binks."

After arriving in Milwaukee and his stint with the Brewers, Wolf quietly solidified a pitching staff that was among one of the best in baseball.

"I've always worked hard," Wolf says. "When I was younger I knew the kind of dedication it takes to be successful. I worked hard to become a better player."

Wolf was drafted by the Dodgers in the 25th round of the 1994 MLB draft, but didn't sign. In 1997 he signed with the Phillies and impressed the brass with a quick rise through the minors.

Making his Major League debut with Philadelphia in June of 1999 against the Blue Jays, Wolf earned his first win. His best full season was with the Phillies in 2003 where he went 16-10 with a 4.23 ERA.

Wolf says in terms of collective demeanor, a team has to set their sights early, and as Legendary Packers Coach Vince Lombardi once says, act like they've been there before.

"You've got to envision success, a championship from day one," Wolf says. "When I was with the Dodgers, we made it into the playoffs. We didn't think 'if' we get to the playoffs, it was 'when' we get to the playoffs."

Despite the huge paydays for pitchers, life on the mound can vary from day to day. Some days you feel invincible and others as vulnerable as a rabbit in a lion's cage.

"You don't know how things are going to go until you're out there," he says.. "I've had days where I felt great and that didn't translate to a good outing."

When things don't feel right, Wolf says you throw until it does.

"I've had to make adjustments right on the mound to find the groove. Some days you can't get the ball to do what you want and others you have to find a way to make it work."

He says it works the other way too, where he doesn't have his best stuff but still has a good outing. Anybody who has watched a game on television or listened on the radio has heard about the 'zone.' The zone to a batter is when the ball looks as big as a grapefruit coming toward the plate. For a pitcher, the zone is when he's throwing 'aspirin tablets' and has amazing command of his pitches.

"Yeah, there is a 'zone,'" Wolf says. "There are some nights you feel everything perfectly. You can manipulate your pitches."

Wolf says he, like every other pitcher, has to take each situation as it comes. Read it as it happens.

"I'll look at a hitter and know he has been hitting my curve ball, but not my slider," he says. "I have to play the percentages."

He says sometimes he has his great stuff and batters are still getting on base. "I'll go with the pitches that give the largest margin for error," he says.

When fans watch a pitcher on the mound they'll often see him shake his head and reject a catcher's signal, or call for a particular pitch. Wolf says it's not about just shaking the catcher off.

"We sit down and talk about a game plan. The other team reacts differently on different nights too, so it's a crap shoot. I ultimately call my own game."

As a Major League veteran, Wolf says he welcomes it when some of the younger pitchers come to ask him some advice.

"I know I did it with the more established pitchers in L.A. and Philadelphia," he says. When he was cutting his teeth in the big leagues, he respected the pitching staff of the Atlanta Braves that featured John Smoltz, Greg Maddux and Tom Glavine.

"Maddux had a way of regaining control and momentum of a game," Wolf says. "If it was bases loaded and no outs, Maddux would walk off the mound and regroup. Reboot his computer, so to speak. In that way he took it back."

In between starts, Wolf likes to relax with a good book. Right now he's reading 'The Hidden Reality,' a book which explores the concept of the multi-universe and the possibility of parallel universes.

"I'm kind of reading weird stuff," he says. "But I like it."

MARK CIARDI

Some people were born lucky. Others, like Mark Ciardi, were born really lucky.

Ciardi is a former Brewers pitcher who won the genetic lottery and parlayed that golden DNA into the big leagues. These days he's a producer for films such as 'Secretariat,' 'The Rookie,' 'Million Dollar Arm.'

He's as handsome as the day is long. With chiseled features he was summoned in front of the camera for a few 7-Up commercials in the mid-80s while other less hunk-like players donated blood to get by. Ciardi is so handsome he prompted Narcissus to get a nip-tuck.

"Everyone assumed we were making so much money in the minors," Ciardi says. "The commercials were a way to help make ends meet."

Born in New Brunswick, New Jersey, the 55-year old Ciardi attended the University of Maryland before being drafted by the Brewers in 1983. He earned a big league promotion in 1987 – a dream come true for Ciardi.

"You kind of keep playing for the sake of playing," he says. "First you make your high school team, and if you're lucky you play after that. Not many get to play after that. I always loved walking out onto the field in front of 30,000 fans."

He was in the Major Leagues less than a month and while it may have been the most thrilling 23 days, Ciardi says he had only one regret.

"I missed the team photo," Ciardi says. "That's one of the things I'd like to get back and have another chance with.

"My time in Milwaukee is kind of a blur. If you didn't know, I was the guy who pitched when we ended the 13-game win streak in 1987."

Ciardi appeared in just four games with 'Team Streak.' He made his big league debut on April 9 at County Stadium – a game the Brewers won 12-11 over Boston on a B.J. Surhoff home run. His next appearance was on April 14 in which he made his starting debut at Baltimore. He pitched five innings and earned a 7-4 victory to help the Brewers run their winning streak to 8-0. The next day, Juan Nieves tossed Milwaukee's first and only no-hitter.

Seven days later, Ciardi made another start. The night before, the Brewers had set a Major League record by rallying to earn their 13th straight win. But when Ciardi took the mound on April 21, the magical carpet ride came to a halt as he took a 7-1 loss at Chicago.

Most fans don't recall the game he won but trivia buffs will remember he was the pitcher of record when the Brewers jackrabbit start came to an end.

While that particular loss remains a rather dubious distinction, Ciardi never let it affect him to the point where he was soured on that season. He still runs across former teammates on occasion.

"Paul Molitor and Robin Yount were very nice to me," he says. "Keep in mind I was just a rookie. I've run into both over the years and it has been great to catch up."

Before he came to the Majors, his agent was very excited about Los Angeles and felt it would be a good fit for Ciardi.

"I moved out to Los Angeles to get ready for a big league camp. That was the first time I ever lived out here in Los Angeles." Ciardi had only visited before and stayed with some friends, other ballplayers.

"L.A. became my home away from home."

Ciardi says he knew some guys who had a bit of success in movies. "My buddy asked what I was going to do after baseball," he recalled. "I never thought it would be film; we didn't have any experience."

While closing out his baseball career in the Minor Leagues, Ciardi started to experience shoulder problems and began thinking about other options. He met Gordon Gray and together they went into the movie business. And why not; they were in Hollywood.

Gray and Ciardi never took the traditional route to filmmaking. No late night viewing of obscure films on the campus, they didn't check out 8 mm cameras from the film department warehouse or have to sit through Citizen Kane four times.

"Not at all," Ciardi says. "We didn't have to do any of that."

Ciardi and Gray started working out of a garage, looking for projects.

"I remember writing a lot of checks," he says. "When you're younger you don't really see all the obstacles. I knew I didn't want to sit behind a desk and ascend the ladder that way." Ciardi says he was fortunate to have access to different people in various industries and says at first he really didn't have a lot of desire to go into the film business. For one thing, he didn't think it was really possible.

Sometimes things go in a direction over which you have little control and Ciardi began to engage in a different kind of pitching. Not from the mound, but for projects. "I was able to talk directly with a lot of studio executives," he says.

"We got a hold of some good material and that entails some luck."

Their first big break was 'The Rookie' based on real-life former MLB pitcher Jim Morris. Ciardi knew about Morris and was familiar with his unique story.

"I read a little piece in Sports Illustrated about Jim," Ciardi says.

Devout Brewers fans might remember Morris was the Brewers' first selection in the 1983 January Draft (Secondary Phase), who pitched at Beloit in 1984 before several arm injuries ended his career in 1989.

After years of coaching high school baseball in Texas, he returned to professional baseball promising his players he'd try out for a big league club if they won the state championship. They did.

Morris impressed Tampa Bay enough to earn a contract. He got a September call up in 1999 and opened the 2000 season with the Devil Rays.

Morris wrote a book about his incredible experiences, a book Ciardi knew would speak to a lot of people if he could make it into a film. He quickly called Ciardi back after a few messages were left.

"I wanted to know if anyone had optioned his book," Ciardi asked. "I thought I could get it in front of the right people."

Ciardi made the film, which still enjoys a solid reputation in the industry and is a great first effort for any producer.

Ciardi and Gray went on to produce a couple more sports-themed movies including, 'Miracle,' a film about the 1980 U.S. Olympic Hockey Team.

"It was a great script," Ciardi added. "The Rookie might be my favorite piece because it's so special to me, but 'Miracle' was special to a lot of people."

He's rather doubtful about a couple of young guys being able to accomplish things he's accomplished out of a garage. "Maybe, but it'd be a tough road. Looking back we were fortunate. I didn't realize it would take two and a half years of my life to make a movie.

Ciardi says the film business, like professional baseball, does indeed get your adrenaline going. Last year Ciardi and his Mayhem Productions added "Secretariat" to his stable of films. Gray and Ciardi also shepherded "Tooth Fairy," "Game Plan," and "Invincible," to the big screen. These are good films which have secured a place in moviegoers hearts.

"It takes years to get a project going and when it does you can really feel the surge," Ciardi says. "A walk on four pitches and a walk on the red carpet aren't that different after all."

Ciardi says he always enjoyed his time in Milwaukee and is looking forward to bringing his wife and children to Miller Park for the first time this summer.

MANNY PARRA

It's good to be Manny Parra. If a man could wave a magic wand and be anyone he wanted, it's a good bet he'd end up as Parra.

He's young, a world-class athlete, handsome and a starting pitcher on a Major League club. He even pitched a perfect game in just his second Triple-A start.

"I'd have to say it's still the best night of my life," the 25-year-old says recently. "Of course my professional debut was also great."

Parra was Milwaukee's 26th round selection in the 2001 First-Year Player Draft. While climbing through the Minor League ranks, he chalked up a 38-19 record posting a 3.05 ERA .

"I think each time you go out to the mound you're looking for something to boost your confidence," Parra says. "You're always looking to move it forward, building upon your previous outing."

Growing up in Carmichael, California, Parra admired the command of Greg Maddux, but idolized the raw power of Randy Johnson.

"Johnson is in a batter's head before he throws his first pitch," Parra says. "His stature is intimidating, the speed of his pitches are intimidating. Batters come to the plate thinking, 'man, I'm facing Randy Johnson.'"

Parra says when a pitcher brings that kind of clout to the mound it's undoubtedly a huge advantage. He added that a batter can't underestimate the kind of damage a pitcher like Johnson can do.

"When we faced Randy in Arizona," he recalled, "he didn't have his good stuff, but it was still

Randy Johnson."

One of the more perplexing components of a pitcher's professional life is whether they have 'it' when they take the mound. What exactly 'it' is may be open to interpretation.

"Some nights you just know when you have 'it,'" Parra says. "It's a nebulous thing that's difficult to describe once it's found. There's a lot of pressure to perform at this level. It's our dream to be up here. I know what I have to do day in and day out to stay here. Just stick to what I've been doing and what's been getting results."

Former Brewer pitching coach Mike Maddux, now pitching coach with the Nationals, said he used to keep a close eye on Parra's progress.

"We were very pleased with the way Manny had been pitching," Maddox says. "He's made a lot of progress. It takes a lot of time on the mound to gain command of your pitches and fortunately he's getting a chance to work on his command in game conditions."

Having command on the mound and consistent execution with pitches has earned him respect, not only from his teammates but also the opposition and the men in blue.

"You can throw well, throw a nasty curve, but if it doesn't hit your location, you can't say you have command," he says. "You're not in command of that pitch.

"You earn more respect with the umpires if you don't give them trouble or try to show them up. The only perfect way to call pitches would be with a computer, but that's not going to happen any time soon. It's a human factor thing. Sometimes they're going to miss a call."

Once again, Parra shows wisdom beyond his years.

"I give a lot of credit to my father for my behavior and attitudes," Parra says. "We didn't have the easiest life growing up but after I signed professionally, things got better for my family. I realize how lucky I am all the time.

"On a recent flight to Atlanta I was thinking I was going to be playing in the same stadium I watched on television during my childhood. The same field as the Braves I grew up with. It's a reality check when you realize this isn't your average job and I think it helps you stay in the moment. Helps you appreciate what you've been blessed with."

Preparation is a huge part of a pitcher's repertoire. Parra is no different.

"When I think of the next series, I always consider adjustments I must make," Parra added. "I'm not talking about on the mound adjustments because I think that's an area a pitcher should leave alone once he takes the mound. You have your mechanics, that's something locked in your mind. You may make adjustments as to how you pitch a certain hitter, control the tempo or slow it down."

The key to pitching is the understanding you can throw well and still get knocked around. The mental portion of the job may be the toughest.

"That's the way I've felt at times," Parra says. "It's almost as though you didn't see it coming. You feel good, you're making your pitches, then all of a sudden you look up at the board and you're down five runs.

"Things at this level happen so quickly. The hitters, the runners and at times I don't understand how or why something happened. That's when I have to do my best to slow things down."

Parra played with current Yankee CC Sabathia and learned a lot from him.

"He doesn't do much to hurt himself on the mound," Parra says. "He has such confidence in everything he does. I ask a lot of questions about what he does in certain situations. He has the confidence on the mound, in the clubhouse, everywhere. You can't help but feed off that kind of confidence."

Parra has an idea of what his baseball legacy should include.

"I'd like to be known as a pitcher who had a lot of power from the left side, able to keep hitters off balance, a guy who knew how to get strikes when he needed them."

LATROY HAWKINS

It would have taken something remarkably alarming to disrupt the cool demeanor of relief pitcher LaTroy Hawkins. A firecracker under his chair or a rattlesnake in his suitcase might do it, but don't bet on it. Hawkins is as cool as absolute zero.

In the Brewers' clubhouse, Hawkins' locker could be found in between two other players with ice in their veins – Ryan Braun and Randy Wolf. Locker assignments and how they come about are a mystery, but it's interesting that Hawkins was placed in between two of the younger stars of the game. It's kind of like having Yoda as a locker mate, except that Hawkins is much taller.

At 6-foot-6, Hawkins comes from Gary, Indiana – Hoosier Country – and his heart was naturally planted under a rim on the hardwood.

"I always had hoop dreams," Hawkins smiled, thereby silently admitting his love for basketball.

His son plays competitive basketball but Hawkins scoffs at the notion that his son is equal to his own youthful talents.

"He's not half the player I was," Hawkins chuckles. "He grew up too easy. Sometimes growing up harder makes you a better player."

Hawkins' wife, Anita, and kids, Dakari and Troi, now live in Dallas, Texas, but playing for Milwaukee allowed him to get back to be able to still visit other members of his family and friends in Gary.

He sees his mother often, and when he does, there is a ritual.

"I say hello and then go right for the fridge," he says. "My mother is a great cook, but my wife is, too."

Nice save.

While excelling in both baseball and basketball, Hawkins says it was his grandfather who urged him to play baseball over basketball.

"He was a genius," he says of his grandfather. "He told me I'd have a better chance making it in baseball."

Hawkins says his grandfather told him he didn't have to be the biggest or the fastest to play baseball, but being mentally tough was what mattered.

Hawkins has a wealth of information to share with younger pitchers and players. Hawkins got the chance to perfect his trade with some legends.

"I learned a lot from Kevin Tapani, Bob Tewksbury," Hawkins says. "I learned from guys like that on how to be a professional, how to grind it out and hone the craft."

He says teammates will tune into him for advice, but he doesn't walk around acting like he knows more than anyone else.

"If I know something, it's because I've been around a long time and can help another pitcher," he added. "We're a tight-knit group in the bullpen, all together. When you make a fist, you need all the fingers and the thumb. We come together in our 'brotherhood.'"

Hawkins was wearing his 'Brotherhood' sweatshirt in the clubhouse during this interview and seemed to mean what he says. "What do you do when you punch? You make a fist and if one of those fingers or the thumb isn't bound together, you can hurt yourself. We're always out there with each other."

So much so, Hawkins says even when he doesn't take the mound in a game, he feels like he pitched. "When one of our guys is on the mound, we feel it, we envision every pitch," he says. "It's almost like a sixth sense we feel with each other."

The life of a relief pitcher is filled with a lot of 'hurry up and wait' days – never knowing if you're going to play; a life much like a box of chocolates – never knowing what you're going to get.

"I'll spend the first four innings in the clubhouse watching the game on television," Hawkins says. "I get a feel for the pitchers and what they're throwing. Keep an eye on the starters' pitch count."

When Hawkins leaves the clubhouse in the fourth inning to go out to the field, that's when he says he's 'locked in.'

As a pitcher, he never physically feels the same way from day to day, explaining that no one in the clubhouse is ever completely healthy.

"They've all got some nagging injuries or pains," he points out, gesturing to the other men in the clubhouse. "It's a mental game and only the toughest survive."

As an athlete acutely aware of his own body, Hawkins says he knows from the moment he wakes up the type of day he's in for.

"When my feet hit the floor out of bed, I know," he says. "As a player ages, he knows when he needs a little rest. If it's going to hurt the team if you're out there, you'd better talk to the manager. If I pitch three days in a row, I know I'm going to feel it."

Like most pitchers who experience injury or arm trouble in their careers, Hawkins went on the disabled list twice in 2010. It's hard enough to recover from arm surgery when you're 29-years- old, much less than 39-years-old. Hawkins had arthroscopic surgery on his right shoulder last year to 'clean up 'his labrum. "The injury didn't happen overnight," Hawkins says. He says his orthopedic specialist, Dr. Lewis Yocum, was confident he'd come back strong.

"Dr. Yocum assured me I'd come back," he says. "I don't think my injury was as serious as some other guy's injuries."

Hawkins says Brewers' Head Trainer Roger Caplinger was one of the constant influences in his recovery.

"Since day one he told me we didn't need to push it," he added. "He stayed on me and developed a plan we both stuck to. He called me every day and stayed in touch."

"To LaTroy's credit, he was very diligent to get back to this level," Caplinger says. "Some people aren't able to do what he did."

Despite the surgery, Hawkins says his fastball is still his 'out' pitch. Craig Counsell's locker was near Hawkins'during Counsell's playing days and Hawkins mentions his admiration for Counsell's abilities.

"He was a great player," Hawkins says of his former teammate. "That's a guy who knows the strike zone." When I asked how he'd approach Counsell at the plate, Hawkins smiled,

"Fastballs. He's going to have to hit my best pitch."

Hawkins was treated like a villain by Cubs fans when he pitched for Chicago. Despite having great numbers in 2004, he blew nine saves down the stretch and fans never forgave him. "I had some tough times in Chicago," Hawkins says, "but I love the city. I think my time in Chicago made me a better player, taught me how to face adversity."

Sometimes fans think they care more about the game than the players do. It's not like a guy wants to give up a home run to lose the game – he wants to win more than anybody.

"You can't show your emotions on the field," Hawkins says. "That's part of the game, especially for a pitcher. Baseball is built on that ritual. You've got to have good people around you from the beginning, smart people who can look out for you. My agent, Larry Reynolds, has always been there for me, always guided me well."

When he's not working, Hawkins says he likes to hang out with the family and watch movies, take a nap on the couch.

"It doesn't really matter which movie, as long as the family is together. I'll play basketball once in a while, read a book," he says. "I may get four or five pages in before I conk out. On the plane I get a few pages in now and then. I complain about a lot of things, but you'll never hear me complain about baseball. Baseball has been very good to me."

BILL WEGMAN

There are angels in the outfield, and sometimes, they fly over the pitcher's mound.

Former Brewers' hurler Bill Wegman sees life in very simple terms.

"It's all about faith and acting in a manner that will keep you in the light of God," he believes and professes these days as a preacher for Impact Church in his hometown of Cincinnati. During his playing career, Wegman may have been experiencing the duality of man. He enjoyed the prestige and luxury of a Major League ballplayer. But he also felt a higher calling.

Brewers fans may remember Wegman for his pitching prowess and a stellar 15-year career with the organization – five in the Minor Leagues and 10 with the big league Club. With the Brewers, the big right-hander won 81 games highlighted by his 1991 campaign in which he posted a 15-7 record and a sparkling 2.84 earned run average. He earned the Hutch Award given to a player who best exemplifies the fighting spirit and competitive desire of Fred Hutchinson.

Selected as an infielder by the Brewers in the fifth round of the 1981 amateur draft, Wegman was converted to a pitcher.

"The Brewers told me they were going to make me a pitcher because of my size (6'5") and arm strength (blazing)," he says. "The higher I went in the minors the more I learned."

He began to show what he was capable of with Class A Beloit when he won 12 Midwest League games in 1982. The following season at Class A Stockton, the Brewers Brass believed they had something when he posted career bests with a 16-3 mark and 1.30 ERA in the California League.

After winning 49 games in the Minor Leagues, Wegman got his shot with a September call-up in 1985. He pitched so well – recording two wins in three outings –he earned a permanent spot in the rotation for the next seven years.

But along the way, he realized something was still missing in his life.

"I had no faith when my career started," Wegman says. "I didn't become a Christian until 1988 in Milwaukee. I was 26-years-old and I thought I had it pretty good. A pastor asked me if I knew Jesus Christ. I shot back at him saying I'm a good person, I don't try to hurt people, unless it's necessary. I have some flaws."

That's when the pastor asked Wegman if he were to appear in front of God at that moment would all that be enough.

"The pastor says Jesus is the way and I chose to pursue him," he reflected. "I realized if I hadn't murdered someone, if I didn't steal or covet, that wasn't going to be enough."

It was then that he dedicated his life to Christ and his stewardship. Wegman says the transition to faith wasn't so much a lightning bolt as a process.

"I had seen my wife (Kim) growing her relationship with Christ," he says. "I saw her peace and I guess that was as close to a lightning bolt I experienced."

There's no bigger stage than the big leagues, but he didn't have peace. "I was very skeptical of 'born again' Christians," he added. "I figured if you needed Jesus as a crutch that was your problem."

It all came down to whether he wanted to know truth. Wegman says that man is faced with temptations throughout his life.

"The motto moving through the baseball ranks was 'play hard on the field and off the field," he says. "At the time my life was what I thought it should be. I didn't have a moral compass."

Sometimes wealthy athletes face a more difficult path than the rest of us.

"If someone is telling you you're a 'god,' you start to believe them," Wegman says. "You're serving yourself. The world is telling you a lie. I got to that point and saw I had no peace and joy. I thought, hey I'm a big-leaguer."

Wegman says what he needed was perspective. "I didn't come by this because it was the obvious choice," he added. "I knew this was my path because it was written. It was prophecy. The evidence in scripture is true."

Life throws you its share of complications, stresses, but Wegman sees things more clearly than most and doesn't blame a supreme being.

"If we'd listened to God in the first place, we wouldn't have these problems," Wegman says. "A lot of bad things do take place but they're a result of sin. When we fell the world fell."

Wegman once commented he thought he was born to be a Major Leaguer. After all, his neighborhood seemed to be full of them. His father used to compete against one of the best the game ever produced.

"In Cincinnati we had a few guys from the same block," he says. "There was Pete Rose and a couple of other guys."

Wegman says he's the kind of guy that always played by the rules and pushed himself.

"I wanted to be the best off the field too," he says. "I think a lot of people around me appreciated the effort. I wanted to be in the best shape, the best competitor."

Wegman says he loved playing for the Brewers and the fans. "It's a lot like Cincinnati," he says. "People from both cities love baseball and beer. For me, Milwaukee had faithful fans, true fans. Folks that appreciated the effort."

Cal Eldred was one of his closest friends and favorite players. "When he came into the big leagues, I would judge people by their work ethic. He was the first guy in my career that could actually outwork me."

Wegman says one of his fondest memories in Milwaukee was dealing with Bud Selig.

"Not because he was the owner of the team and was paying me," Wegman says. "I really liked him because he appreciated my efforts. I only spoke with him three or four times during my entire time with the Brewers but he told me I was going to be around for awhile."

Wegman says being an ex-big leaguer has been a strong platform for reaching people.

"I was absolutely determined to make it in another way," he says. "The reason I can speak with authority and passion is I believe with all my heart, soul and strength this is the purpose of my life."

DAVE BALDWIN

As a kid, Dave Baldwin was one of the brightest in the neighborhood. That's not bragging, just fact. As a young adult, he was one of the most cerebral guys to ever pick up a resin bag and pitch inside the lines on a Major League Baseball field.

His intellect has the movement of a slider and the vigor of a 100-mph fastball. Baldwin pitched in the Major Leagues from 1959 until 1974 and played alongside some of the legends of the game. He played in Washington with the Senators, then in Milwaukee, and afterwards the White Sox. In 176 career appearances, he was considered strictly a relief specialist, posting a 6-11 record and a 3.08 ERA. He managed 22 saves – all but one with the Senators.

When he pitched, Baldwin says he was cognizant of the physics in the game, but didn't dwell on those things when he was on the mound. He did what any pitcher must do when facing a professional hitter – he cleared his head and focused on the batter.

"I remember as a kid learning about Magnus Force," Baldwin says. "It was named after a guy named Gustav Magnus who studied the curvature of cannon balls, and that lent itself to the study of baseballs." He says knowing about the physics, however didn't affect him one way or the other when he was on the mound.

Baldwin didn't learn to play baseball on the streets of Brooklyn or on a suburban field. Rather, he honed his skills on the sand-covered terrain of Arizona. Like most kids, Baldwin always believed he'd be a Major League pitcher one day. "It was my first goal all along," he added.

Growing up in Tucson, he says he and his friends played all year long because of the cooperative weather.

"We didn't like to play sports like football and basketball where the ball could be punctured by cactus," Baldwin smiled, mentioning that when you needed a field you just pushed the sand around until you had a diamond and called it a ball field.

As a kid, the Cleveland Indians trained in Tucson, and his parents would allow him to skip school to go to games. That's a little surprising given that both his parents were teachers.

"In those days you could walk right up to the players," Baldwin recalled. "I'd watch Bob Feller and Bob Lemon warming up. I'd go home and imitate them. That's how I learned to pitch." If you're going to emulate a pitcher, those guys are as good as any."

Now 77 years old, Baldwin has made Yachats, Oregon, his home these last eight years. He's a scientist and studies the chromosomes of fruit flies and how they behave.

"We're examining how genes are turned on and off," he says. "Humans share a lot of genes with fruit flies." The man made a deft segue from fly balls to fruit flies.

As Baldwin says on his website, he's the only geneticist and only systems engineer ever to play Major League Baseball. He's been published in *Proceedings of the Entomological Society of Washington,* a publication so erudite most of us have never heard of the publication.

PhDs and scholarly writing may seem quite a jump from pitching, so let's go back and retrace his steps. Baldwin was working towards his undergraduate degree at the University of Arizona while playing professional ball. He completed his undergraduate degree when his career ended, then went on to earn his PhD in genetics and worked in the field for a couple of years. Baldwin had planned to become a professor to teach and engage in research, but that didn't come to past.

"I discovered baby boomers had moved through the university system and there were no jobs open," he says. "But I did work in the field for a couple of years."

In other words, life threw him a change-up. Undaunted, the scholarly man went back to school and earned a masters in systems engineering. Today he may be out of the game, but he never seems to be too far away from it either. In his career, Baldwin has studied the action of the pop-up in baseball.

"If you'll notice, infielders have an awful time with sky-high pop-ups," he says. "Sometimes they'll miss it by five feet. That's because they're tough to judge. The ball does a loop towards the outfield then comes back towards the infield. It looks a lot easier than it actually is."

Baldwin also collaborated on a paper about the 'vertical sweet' of the bat, or the 'sweet spot,' as many players refer to the zone in the middle of the bat.

"It's the place where you get the best wood on the ball," he offered. "Just looking at the vertical dimensions of that is fascinating. If you hit the ball a little low, you're going to hit it up. If you hit it too high, it results in a ground ball and probably an out."

Baldwin is the author of *Snake Jazz*, a book about his career in the game. Baldwin says 'snake jazz' is a term for a pitch that hangs, wavers, dives and slides. He says a batter will come back to the dugout after striking out and say to the manager, 'man, he never threw a fastball, just all that snake jazz.'

A particularly intriguing chapter is "Batter Psychology 101," in which Baldwin examines how he would face Babe Ruth and leads the reader through the sequence of pitches he would throw, complete with a pitch-by-pitch assessment and explanation.

One of the topics Baldwin writes about in *Snake Jazz* is the salary discrepancies between current players and those when he played.

"One man today can earn as much as the entire league did back then." When Baldwin pitched, he says most players earned what most blue collar workers earn today. "Pitchers were probably treated with less respect than the other players," he says, in complete contrast to today's baseball world where pitchers are treated as well, if not better, than most other players. "It's all about entertainment. It's what we as a society value most. We have rock stars and so-forth, so why shouldn't the athletes get paid the same?"

As an educated guy who pitched in the 'bigs,' Baldwin is in a pretty good position to assess the demise of a pitcher's abilities.

"Some guys just fail to get it over the plate when they need to," Baldwin says. "It's not arm strength. I think some just try to throw too hard like they have to be even better in the Majors." Baldwin was primarily a sinker ball pitcher and says the pressure to throw extremely hard wasn't something he had to deal with.

"I never had a 100 mph fastball," he confesses. "You see quite a few guys who fall off the map when they're doing extremely well. Some guys did extremely well in the minors but end up with just a cup of coffee in the Major Leagues."

Baseball broadcasters like to talk about a pitcher 'having his stuff,' in one game, and 'not having his good stuff' in another? What does Baldwin see as the reason? "In my opinion it's usually because a pitcher has lost some of his coordination for that day and he's just not throwing the ball where he should," he says.

"Your arm has to come around at just the right time, every time, for you to be successful. That's not always easy to do.

Baldwin spent his career in the American League including a stint with the Brewers in 1970, where he posted a solid 2.55 ERA as a reliever. In 28 games, he was 2-1 with one save. He didn't run to the mound from the outfield when he got the call, nor did he spend a lot of time trying to intimidate the hitter. "I just simply paid attention to the game situation, what would be going on when I got in there," he described.

"Other than that I really didn't try to psyche myself up."

Baldwin says today's pitchers are perhaps more mentally tough than when he played.

"Mental toughness really can't be underestimated," he began. "When I pitched, we were counting on overpowering hitters. Today's pitchers are developing more pitches. They're throwing no-hitters. When you have more than one pitch, a pitcher has got to do a lot more thinking on the mound."

The first game Baldwin pitched in the big leagues was against the Tigers – a powerful lineup which included Al Kaline and Norm Cash, a couple of guys who could make a pitcher shake in his cleats.

"I told myself they're just the same as other batters, just one more guy to get out," Baldwin says. "I didn't pitch to avoid hitters' strengths. Instead I pitched to my own strengths. If a hitter was a good low ball hitter, he was going to get my pitch, a sinker."

According to Baldwin, sports can be an important component to many people's lives.

"Fans are having fun," he says. "They look to baseball as a release and a departure from their everyday life."

Baldwin says he has too many things on his plate to really pay attention to baseball these days, but he still keeps his hand in the dynamics of the game.

"I don't really follow the game much anymore, but I am collaborating with some scientists," he says. "I've written a number of articles on the physics of baseball."

Baldwin remembers Milwaukee well as he came with the Pilots from Seattle when the team suddenly moved and became the Brewers. "It was funny, because most of us had already sent our families on to Seattle," Baldwin says.

"Dick Ellsworth, Bob Humphries and I were called upon to solidify the bullpen. We got out of last place, which was a good thing."

Baldwin now takes an annual trek to Safeco Field to a Mariners' game.

"One of my friends is a V.P. with the Mariners and he gets us seats anywhere we want to sit," he says. "It's really a lot of fun."

He says the atmosphere around the game has changed dramatically, as he talked about the Golden Age of Baseball and his memories of Satchel Paige and Sandy Koufax.

"I knew Koufax," Baldwin says. "My roommate with the Senators, Doug Camilli, had been Koufax's roommate with the Dodgers. Whenever we went to Los Angeles, we had lunch with him. I know he has a reputation of being somewhat reclusive, but at lunch he was very outgoing."

Late in his career, Baldwin played in Hawaii in the Pacific Coast League and says the fans were similar to those in the golden days of baseball. "They'd bring you pineapples and bread," he says. "It was a special experience."

When he's not working with fruit flies or analyzing pop-ups, Baldwin enjoys what the Pacific Coast has to offer.

"We've got hiking trails all over the place," he says. "The ocean is far enough down below that we're not worried about getting washed away." These days Baldwin doesn't watch television or even get the newspaper.

"I'm happier than I've ever been," he admitted. "I think I got that competitiveness out of my system."

JIM LONBORG

He left the bright lights of a large historical city, came to the Midwest and had arguably the best season of his career.

Jim Lonborg had a long and distinguished life in professional baseball. He spent 15 years on three Major Leagues rosters including the Red Sox (1965-71), the Brewers (1972) and the Phillies (1973-79). When all was says and done, he found his way into the Red Sox Hall of Fame in 2002.

But he has had another successful career away from the game, spending nearly 30 years as a practicing dentist in Massachusetts.

"I was driving with my wife Elizabeth, and she turned to me and says, 'why don't you become a dentist,'" says Lonborg, a Stanford University graduate, who pondered about life after baseball. "Simple as that."

Lonborg took his wife's suggestion to heart and attended the Tufts University Dental School and has worked in the profession in Hanover, Massachusetts ever since.

Signed as a free agent in 1963, Lonborg won the Cy Young Award as a member of the Red Sox '1967 Impossible Dream Team' that won the American League Championship and lost to Bob Gibson and the St. Louis Cardinals in the World Series.

That season, Lonborg posted an AL best 22-9 record with 246 strikeouts.

Five years later, he was part of one of the biggest trades in Brewers history when he came to Milwaukee along with George Scott, Billy Conigliaro, Joe Lahoud, Ken Brett and Don Pavletich from Boston for Marty Pattin, Lew Krausse, Tommy Harper and Pat Skrable.

"My best ERA was in Milwaukee," Lonborg says of his 2.83 ERA in 223 innings pitched in 1972. He also fanned 143 batters. "I liked my time with Bud Selig and see him on occasion at different functions."

Among his 30 starts with the Brewers, Lonborg managed a Club-leading 11 complete games and 14-12 record to go along with a pair of shutouts for a team that won only 65 games.

After just one season in a Brewers uniform, Lonborg was dealt to Philadelphia along with Sanders, Brett and Earl Stephenson for Don Money, John Vukovich and Bill Champion.

Early in his career he was tagged 'Gentleman Jim,' and some say it was because of his fearlessness for pitching on the inside of the plate, thus making it a sarcastic moniker. Others claim it was because he was kind to members of the media. While both may be valid, Lonborg says what he felt was the impetus for the nickname.

"I made a living coming inside on hitters," Lonborg says. He doesn't believe his approachable behavior with the press was the reason for nickname.

Lonborg says he had enough power to pitch inside and players learned quickly to respect that power. In his era pitchers finished games and racked up a ton of innings.

"More guys are throwing harder than most of us did back then," Lonborg says. "Part of it is certainly genetic but some could be attributed to the incredible amount of training these guys do today."

He dismissed the notion today's players are getting star treatment.

"I don't know if the strike zone is shrinking," Lonborg says. "I think it's more of hitters getting more leeway in responding to pitches inside. A pitcher must 'deserve' to get a particular call, in my opinion."

Lonborg was a student of the game and life. He comes by the proclivity towards education honestly.

"My father was a professor of agriculture at California Polytechnic," he says. "He was a great track runner. I guess good genes." His mother Elizabeth was in television. "She had one of the early evening news shows," he pointed out.

You might imagine fingers that used to throw a curve ball would seem odd near your mouth, testing the density of your molars.

"It hasn't been much of an issue," Lonborg says. "Anybody that's in the healthcare field sees the patient as their primary focus and I think it works the other way too."

He says he wants people to come to his office because they have faith in his abilities, not his ability to throw a wicked slider.

"My career in baseball has helped to break the ice and make people feel comfortable," Lonborg says, "especially patients who like baseball."

His practice is near Fenway Park and he tries to take in a game once a month. "They're very good to former players," he says of the Red Sox management. "They let me sit in the Legend's Suites. There are a lot of former players there who meet guests."

Lonborg considers former teammate and Hall-of-Famer Carl Yastrzemski as a friend. "I always got along with Carl," he acknowledged.

"His biggest problem was being socially uncomfortable. He's a great guy when you get him on his own."

When he's not working, he likes to toil in his garden. Lonborg, now 68, and his wife, have a home in Scituate, Massachusetts. "There are so many beautiful gardens out there."

If you've ever watched the television sitcom Cheers, you may remember the picture behind the bar of owner Sam Malone pitching; it's actually a shot of Lonborg.

"I didn't know they were going to do that," Lonborg says. "They did ask if they could use it, and I says 'absolutely.'"

JIM ABBOTT

Entering the season, there have been 295 no-hitters registered in Major League Baseball history. Of those gems, 20 have been perfect games, nine have involved multiple pitchers and two have come in the postseason. But only one no-hitter, since the first was recorded in 1876, was tossed by a one-armed pitcher.

That one belongs to Jim Abbott, who enjoyed a successful big league career with the Angels, Yankees, White Sox and Brewers, despite being born without a complete right arm.

Overcoming adversity is something we all face. Then there are those individuals, like Abbott, who overcome mind-numbing insurmountable obstacles.

His early years read like a storybook. A stellar high school player in Michigan, who was drafted to play in the big leagues out of high school, he instead opted to get a degree at the University of Michigan. He starred on the baseball team, leading the Wolverines to a pair of Big Ten Championships.

In 1987, Abbott won the prestigious James E. Sullivan Award as the nation's best amateur athlete. The following year, he was the Angels' No. 1 pick in the draft before going on to earn a gold medal in the demonstration event at the 1988 Summer Olympics.

He played in only 22 games in the Minor Leagues but only near the end of his career. He went straight to the big leagues after the Olympics, making his debut on April 8, 1989 against the Mariners. Two weeks later, he earned his first win – a 3-2 decision over the Orioles, and by his seventh start picked up his first complete game – a 5-0 shutout over the Red Sox.

His greatest season came with the Angels when he posted an 18-11 record in 1991. But his most memorable performance came in the New York pinstripes when on September 4, 1993, he pitched a no-hitter against the Indians at Yankee Stadium.

"After the Olympics I was in a Major League locker room looking around at all the veterans, and I was tucked away with all the other young guys," Abbott recently reflected. Looking longingly around that locker room, Abbott says he didn't have any expectations, he just wanted to stay with the Club.

Now, more than 10 years after retiring with the Brewers, Abbott, whose last victory was also a 5-0 shutout on July 5, 1999, says his decision to move on with his life following an 87-win career.

"My wife and I went to Northern Michigan to spend some time to figure out what we were going to do next," Abbott says. "We looked out over Lake Michigan and I decided I didn't want to keep playing. I knew more of what I didn't want to do than what I wanted."

It finally came to him – a motivational speaker. You'd expect Abbott to be a natural, the life of the room.

"That's kind of funny," Abbott quickly responded. "I don't consider myself to be like that. It's rewarding (public speaking) and in some ways I wish I could be a coach. Speaking is a little like coaching, but it took me a while to get comfortable." Abbott says he still gets performance anxiety before speaking. "It's a lot like pitching," he added.

He says his talks are tailored to the particular audience, but it's always his inspirational story at the core. "I'll talk about what they face every day, figure out what part of my message will apply to what they do through the framework of success and failure," Abbott says.

He speaks regularly around the country to a variety of business and educational audiences. "It amazes me," he says. "I can be in Tennessee or Iowa and people remember my career, the way I played. That is part of my story."

He credits his work ethic and adapting to adversity as key components to his success.

"I work so hard at what I do," Abbott says. "But sometimes I think a work ethic can be a symptom of a fear of failure. And that's not necessarily a bad thing.

"My work ethic comes from that. I've never been one of those who runs away."

Abbott says during his motivational talks there are some general terms he narrows down and he focus on an acronym: ADAPT (Adjustability, Determination, Accountability, Perseverance and Trust).

"It's really some general ideas narrowed down," Abbott says. "I think it's about learning to find your own way in whatever field you choose."

Abbott says he gets a lot of letters from kids facing similar adversities physical adversities in their lives.

"I like to tell kids that adjustments are the important thing," he pointed out. "Anybody can work hard but you have to know how to make things work for you. There is also a huge aspect of accountability, making the most out of what you've been given."

He says he's very appreciative of what he accomplished in baseball. "Any time you make the Majors, you've got to be proud," he added. "There were days I didn't think I could have gotten one more stitch of effort out of myself. I sometimes wish I could have developed a better off-speed pitch, a change up."

Abbott says he realized how people think about how their careers will end and how lucky he was to leave on his own terms.

With the absence of a right hand, Abbott says his success on the mound took a lot of practice. "I did practice my fielding a lot, not because I had to make up for something, just because I wanted to be better," he says.

Abbott talked about his time with Angels coach Jimmy Reese. "He told wonderful stories about rooming with Babe Ruth," he began. "Jimmy was a baseball icon (Reese's number '50' was retired by the Angels in 1995).

"Jimmy would grab this fungo bat Reggie Jackson gave me. He could hit a ball wherever he wanted during batting practice. He would hit the ball like a 'come backer,' and we'd do that a lot. That was some of the best fielding practice."

When Abbott was on the mound, opposing teams would often bunt, a practice some might consider unsportsmanlike. But he never looked at it that way.

"I don't remember taking that personally," Abbott says. "If I did it was a mistake. I tried to exploit weaknesses in other players. When you overcame and defeated an obstacle, it was always sweeter. I always looked for solutions to get it done when they says it couldn't be done."

Though he spent only one season in Milwaukee– his last - the franchise and the city made an impression.

"My time in Milwaukee was so quick, but I loved being in the midwest," Abbott says. "I had some good friends, like Jeromy Burnitz and Mark Loretta. I remember Milwaukee fondly, even though I was reconciling the end of my career. I really liked playing for Phil Garner."

Not known for his hitting prowess, Abbott fondly remembers a few clutch plate appearances in a Brewers uniform – the only time he batted during his career.

"My two hits came with the Brewers," he recalled. "Both were off Jon Lieber when he was with the Cubs and both driving in runs. I think I got one hit in Wrigley Field. I didn't have a great average but it's great when you can get a hit. I was glad to have that experience."

Abbott is a man who achieved heights few others have, and accomplishments the rest of us can only dream about.

"Looking back, I gave it everything I had," he says.

As if he were capable of anything else.

MARCUS HANEL

To say Marcus Hanel is just a bullpen catcher is akin to saying the F-35 Lightning is just another airplane. .

Hanel joined the Brewers after retiring as an active player back in 1999. Originally from Racine, the Brewers have utilized the skills of this versatile member of the organization primarily as a critical component in the bullpen, but also as a cohesive force and aide-de-camp in ways most of us will never see.

Hanel can relate to world-class athletes whether on a pristine diamond where they make their living or in the bullpen where he makes his.

"I usually arrive at the park about five or six hours before a night game," Hanel says recently. "Sometimes, I work with the pitchers, other times, I'll run through some drills with the catchers; wherever I'm needed."

With that, Hanel grabbed two huge bags filled with batting practice balls, making the bags seem as light as Styrofoam. His hands are as thick as they are wide after years of catching ear-splitting 95-mph fast balls for a living.

Before a recent game with the Dodgers, Hanel was busy working with catcher Mike Rivera, deliberately throwing pitches into the dirt in front of Rivera to help hone the catcher's ball smothering skills.

At 6-foot-5 and 250 pounds, Hanel appears larger in person. Certainly, a big catcher by anyone's standards - one of the last guys you'd want to have to run through at home plate after rounding third.

"I kind of beat up Mikey with the balls in the

dirt," Hanel says, sounding a bit remorseful about some of the knocks Rivera sustained in the drill.

That's one of the first things you realized about Hanel. His heart is as big as his shoulders.

"I'll help players like Mike work through a drill like that about once per home-stand," he added. "The drill is intended to help keep Rivera in playing shape as he's not getting a lot of starts with Jason Kendall performing so well."

With a permanent smile, Hanel displays a youthful enthusiasm for his job and the game, a quality which undoubtedly keeps in favor with the powers-to-be. He's been with the club longer than most of the coaches, with the exception of Bill Castro.

Hanel goes wherever he's needed before a game, whether it's playing 'long catch' with pitcher Dave Bush, or some pre-game work with Eric Gagne in the bullpen.

"My priority is obviously with the pitchers and working with Mike Maddux," Hanel says. "But I'll throw batting practice and protect the pitchers from line drives while others are hitting fly balls."

The pitching staff has a schedule to keep even on days they're not pitching, and Hanel is instrumental in the process. Pitchers run, throw, take batting practice, and Hanel is with them every step of the way helping the pitchers maintain their edge so they can perform to the best of their abilities during their next outing.

The bullpen is definitely a home away from home for Hanel, who hauls his gear behind the wall in left-center field before each game and he won't leave the area until the game has ended. Those hours are spent with the same group of guys each night, watching and waiting.

"These guys know their roles," Hanel says. "During the early innings it's pretty laid back, guys relaxing, staying loose."

Conversations about anything are fair game; family, golf, what have you. Once the game enters the fifth or sixth inning, Hanel says there is a decidedly different vibe in the bullpen.

"The pitchers know a lot is expected of them," he says. "These guys are real people, they don't want to disappoint."

Relationships in the bullpen are lasting ones. Hanel says former reliever Matt Wise, now with the Mets, kept the bullpen laughing all the time, helping to ease the tension.

"I like Derrick Turnbow a lot," he added. "He took the losses so hard and I don't know if a lot of the fans recognized that fact."

Make no mistake, Hanel is as much a part of the team as anyone else in uniform even if he doesn't take the field during a game.

"I'll talk to Mike Maddux if I feel someone is throwing a little differently, or if I notice something in their motion," Hanel says. "I'll let Mike and Bill know if I see some extra life on the ball, or if it's too high in the zone."

Ballparks, like Miller Park, are a great improvement over some of the older stadiums.

"The pitchers have a large area to stretch in our bullpen," he says. "They have a clear eye-level view of the field and don't have to look through a chain-link fence to catch the action."

Hanel has a refreshing approach and humility in this high powered sport – qualities the Brewers have known about for a long time.

"I'm supportive in everything they do," Hanel says. "I know what I'm here for."

Hanel has a charitable organization called "Koos For Kids" that helps terminally ill and disadvantaged youths in Southeastern Wisconsin.

JOE CRAWFORD

He seems to live and die with every pitch, generally in a figurative sense.

A large man with a big smile, Joe Crawford still looks like a big kid at the age of 44, who'd be more than happy to grab his mitt and go into the game if asked. Instead, he's content to do the next best thing. Now in his seventh season with the Brewers, Crawford assists the coaching staff with on-field instruction and game preparation.

"During the day I may be found shagging B.P. (batting practice)," he says recently. "I might be asked to throw a ball back into the infield for Ryan Braun during warm-ups, protecting his arm."

After that he might be asked to throw batting practice to hitters.

"Having a left-hander throwing batting practice is rather rare in the big leagues," Crawford added.

When his on-field duties are complete, Joe shifts gears. With the first pitch of the game, his expertise requires him to utilize a different set of synapses. It consists of advanced scouting and game review.

When not on the diamond, he's holed up in a special room adjacent to the dugout tunnel where, within a moment's notice, he can provide in-game analysis or pre-and post-game scrutiny.

The area is highly sensitive in many ways. First, there is a boatload of relatively classified information for coaches and players to review. Secondly, it's off limits to media and prying eyes, offering a 'safe zone' for players to examine material, relax and meditate prior to the upcoming game.

"I could plan my day out but it'd be useless," Crawford says. He certainly has the academic credentials, graduating cum laude from Kent State University with a Bachelor of Science degree in finance.

Back in his bunker, Crawford coordinates information between coaches and advance scouts. He earned his stripes in the game playing professionally from 1991-1998, ping-ponging between the Mets and Red Sox and some short stints with the Brewers and Diamondbacks organizations. Joe did pitch a no-hitter in the minors before getting a shot at the show with the Mets in 1997.

Crawford appeared in 19 games and posted a 4-3 record and 3.30 ERA. He earned a victory in his last big league appearance to go out in style.

Crawford tried a stint pitching in Japan with the Chiba Lotte Marines and also served as a pitching coach for the Bridgeport Bluefish of the Atlantic Independent League.

"I think it helps with my relationships with the players to have played in the Major Leagues," he says.

His title is quite long. Before the National Anthem, he is officially a coaching assistant, sporting uniform number 56. Once "Home of the Brave" is belted out, Crawford becomes the Brewers digital media coordinator and disappears from sight into his own domain.

What was that pitch? Where was it? How fast was it? Was it a ball or strike? Did the batter swing? Where did he hit the ball? These are questions Crawford will answer hundreds of times during a game. He then enters each one of the answers into a database the size of a Mac truck.

Players will pick his brain in the middle of an inning.

Crawford tries to be very tactful with his reply.

"A lot of times they'll come in to bend my ear about a pitch or some play on the field," he says. "It's all about being in the moment. They are the ones in the game and I'm not going to disrupt their focus. If they say the pitch was a ball then it was a ball to me too. When cooler heads prevail, usually after the game, they will tend to see a pitch more clearly and sometimes agree with the call."

Crawford says Prince Fielder is very animated when he's in his area during a game.

"He may have disagreed with a call but then he comes in here and sees the umpire was right," he says. "He'll be the first to tip his hat to a pitcher. He's been around the game so long I think he sees things a bit differently."

Others keep things loose.

"Craig Counsell always asks me 'how my personality is today?'" Crawford joked. "There are times things can be stressful. I guess I'm not always as warm as I can be."

Again this speaks to the intensity of his work area. Crawford doesn't wear glasses with tape on the bridge but this room could be considered a techno-geek's paradise. He's surrounded by flat screen monitors, computers, back-up hard drives. Under his electronic canopy he can see multiple angles of players during batting practice, pitchers during warm-ups and just about anything else in Miller Park.

"A lot of this is habit and routine," Crawford began. "I'll have players who come up here while the Brewers are at bat and ask me technical questions while I'm charting a game. It can be challenging. There are so many things going on. Picture yourself trying to write a letter to your wife while writing this article."

Crawford interviewed for a scouting position with the Brewers before sliding behind his bank of computers.

"I think I have a petty strong ability to identify talent and communicate with the players," he says. "

A light bulb must have gone off over Brewers Assistant General Manager Gordon Ash's head when he realized he had an ex-player, someone who was young, trainable and had some technical acumen.

There's a lot of psychology involved in baseball, particularly when examining and dissecting swings.

"It all starts in Spring Training," Crawford says. "I'd say it really starts to ramp up once the roster has been decided. Players start to come in and look at video more so at that point."

During the game he's charting everything. When there's a break in the action, Joe will head into an adjoining room where he's working on data related to opposing teams who the Brewers will face in the coming weeks and months. He coordinates information between coaches so they can plan. He gathers data from advance scouts. It seems like it never ends.

"We have a vault where we keep all our videos from every game in the Majors," he says. "If it happened in a game, we will find it.

"If a guy is rolling he generally won't come in to look at tape. Then again, it's different for everybody. It's a very individual thing and there's not one rule for any one player. They can come in one day, and not the next. Some will come in multiple times a day."

Whether hitters and pitchers are better off with today's technology compared to players from different eras is tough to quantify. But that really doesn't matter. The technology has really become indispensable to players, as ritualistic as putting on a uniform.

"I like coming in here," pitcher Manny Parra says. "If you ask his Crawford's opinion he'll give it to you straight. Some players find that refreshing and others may find it a bit disconcerting. As for me I like that."

According to Crawford, every Major League team is required to provide an area with a live game feed for visiting teams to conduct business on the road.

When the Brewers are home, Crawford doesn't get much time to stay at his apartment.

"I do everything in this clubhouse," he says. "It's home. We spend more time here (in the clubhouse) than anywhere else. In baseball, if you're on time, you're late."

Someday, Crawford would love an opportunity to be a pitching or bullpen coach. But for now, he's happy where he's at.

"I couldn't be in a better place," he smiled. "I'm in the thick of things; I'm in the big leagues."

PAT LISTACH

Pat Listach had good reason to be miffed when he spoke from Des Moines, but he wasn't. For that and other reasons, he seems to be one of the nicer guys I'd met in baseball.

A communications snafu ended up in wrong numbers and phone-tag. I finally got in touch with the clubhouse of the Iowa Cubs, who tracked Listach down for me. It was a bad connection and I asked him if I could try him from another line. I half expected him to just hang up and walk away, but he says it'd be no problem.

In 1992, Listach was named the AL Rookie of the Year. He says he could still recall the ovation from Milwaukee fans after he won the award.

After he left he Brewers, Listach played for the Astros where he and his family make their off-season home. When his playing days ended, baseball recognized Listach had coaching and managerial potential.

"I pride myself on being aware of many facets of the game," Listach says. "Working with the infielders on defense, positioning them, is something I enjoy. I like to work with some of the defensive aspects of the game."

Listach presents a glowing resume in a baseball job interview. The 1992 Rookie of the Year and six season sin the majors. He became the first player in Brewers history to receive the award. This year is the 10th anniversary of Listach's achievement. He seemed surprised the time had passed so quickly.

"Yeah, I guess it has been 10 years," he says quietly.

Listach maintains a friendship with Jim Gantner and recently saw him at spring training. He has what he calls a 'lasting relationship with Laurel and Wendy Prieb and equipment manager and clubhouse director Tony Migliaccio.

Brewers former director of media relations Jon Greenberg is proud to call Listach a friend.

"Pat has always been one of my favorite players in the organization," Greenberg says. "His wife and children couldn't have been nicer. When he won the award we were so excited. We popped a bottle of champagne in his honor."

"I consider him a friend," Migliaccio says. "You see a lot of players that don't necessarily appreciate what they have in the big leagues. Pat was always a guy that treated other s with respect."

Listach says he comes from a close knit family.

"I call my mom in Louisiana once a day. I also keep in touch with the rest of my family on a regular basis." Listach is also a potential for the Louisiana Sports Hall of Fame.

"That's the first I've heard of it," he says. "When I was a kid I went to the ceremony where Lou Brock was inducted into the same club. I didn't get to meet him, I was just a kid."

An old Brewers media guide listed hunting and fishing as a couple of Listach's hobbies.

"Wow, I haven't done either of those in a while. My father passed away two years ago and left me all his gear, his guns and fishing equipment. My son asks me all the time when I'm going to take him hunting."

Like most ballplayers, Listach has traveled around a bit. He went to Houston, now Des Moines, but he still counts Milwaukee as a place he holds a lot of memories.

"I don't think I played as well as I would have liked in Milwaukee because of my injuries. But I was always supported by fans in Milwaukee. One of the highlights of my career was my first at-bat in Milwaukee back in 1993. The crowd gave me a standing ovation; I still get chills from that moment. Other than the birth of my kids that stands out as one of my greatest moments of my life."

Listach hasn't had the opportunity to visit Miller Park but that didn't keep him from stealing a quick peak as the bus drove by on its way to Appleton.

"I made the bus driver pass by Miller Park," Listach says. "It was beautiful."

Laurel Prieb, Brewers vice president of marketing, recalls Listach as a man that holds friendships dear to his heart. Prieb knows Listach as a man who puts family first, as well as those that cheered him on.

"He's one of those guys that always took good care with the fans," Prieb says. "A Major League player could sign autographs from the moment he woke up until bed time and not fill all the requests. But Pat never complained. It's not as easy as people think it is. Pat always made every effort to rise to the occasion and fulfill the expectation of being a Major League player."

The Brewers have a tradition of keeping up good relationships with former players.

"Pat certainly has a place in our history," says Greenberg. "He will never be forgotten. If the opportunity ever presented itself, the organization would definitely consider having Pat as part of our team."

"You can't think of the 92 season without Pat coming to mind," Prieb says. "Pat will always have a place in baseball and we will always have a special place for Pat.

The possibility of someday returning to Milwaukee isn't lost on Listach.

"I'm with the Cubs right now, but I'd always welcome the opportunity to return to Milwaukee. I would have no problem going back."

JERRY ROYSTER

People say it never hurts like you think it will.

A doctor can assure you the injection wont sting and throb, but he's just pulling your chain. You're going to feel it.

Being released from your duties as a Major League manager, regardless of the circumstances, has got to sting. Davey Lopes was fired from his job as manager of the Brewers on April 18th during his third year at the wheel. Management did what was viewed as best for the team after the franchises worst start in history. Bench coach Jerry Royster was named interim manager

Someone or something had to put life into the team before an autopsy was ordered. The players certainly didn't help Lopes' cause, unable to hit with any consistency.

Lopes reacted to the firing the same way to good news that came his way—stern and stoic until the end. He was never known as an easy interview with media but that doesn't mean he was a bad guy. Media can ask a lot of dumb questions. Where lopes may have fallen into a rut is with his players.

Mark Loretta is a utility player with the team and believes some of the players were pressing too hard to impress Lopes. Mike Matheney, a former teammate of Loretta's and current player with the Cardinals agrees.

"I think players go out and play their game and always try to please their manager, no matter who it is," Matheney says. "That's the way I was taught the game. You do what you can to win and part of winning is following the manager's lead."

Royster doesn't buy into the concept of pushing a player too hard to please.

"I don't know how you press too hard to help somebody," Royster says. "I believe if you're standing up at the plate you're trying to get a hit. I don't care what the situation is. They could be bombing two states over and if the game is still being played, you're going to try to get a hit. You've got to relax, play the game. Your natural talents won't come through if you don't."

Brewers legend Cecil Cooper disagrees with Royster.

"You like a guy so well, you're really trying to push to get a hit. You're thinking about issues when you're up there and it clouds your mind. It puts more pressure on you than you should have. When you go to play, you've got to have a free mind. I'm sure pressing too hard happens and I' sure it was happening here."

Royster is in his third season on the Brewers staff. He played for 16 years in the big leagues for five different clubs. From all accounts, including Laurel Prieb, vice president of marketing, Royster is a pleasure to be around.

"I can tell you Jerry is one of those people we all know that when he walks into a room, it makes you happy he's there. Given what is a wonderful personality, an upbeat outlook and someone who just has fun.

Royster's affection and devotion to Lopes is clear. Royster was the student to Lopes' role as professor and they wanted to ensure they had coaches that could go wherever they were needed. He also knows good coaching can only go so far.

"It's hard to play as bad as we played," Royster

says. "Hard to play offense as bad as we played. The players want to come out of that funk as soon as possible. I don't think Davey would have been fired if we played to our ability."

Cooper has faith in Royster's future.

"He really approaches players, talks to them. I know they like him a lot," Cooper says. "He carries himself pretty well. He's always smiling, yet you know he's serious.   I think he has a chance to do well, I really do." Royster assessed the team's start with candor.

"We did everything wrong, even the games we won, we tried not to loose. We're going to play better. We have to play better."

Royster says he did sense a different aura from the players after the change.

"The guys were more realized than they had been. Some felt pretty darn bad and responsible for the firing. It was kind of a solemn clubhouse. Some guys were uncharacteristically quiet. You can tell they felt bad about their part in our failure to win games."

It's going to take that kind of direct approach to instill a sense of responsibility on the part of the players. Managerial changes aren't necessarily a panacea to a team's problems. But it's the most visible action a team can take to own up to them.

In 2014, Royster coached the Shalhevet Firehawks to a 2nd place finish in the Mulholland League.

BRIAN ANDERSON

It's not easy to walk into a role previously played by another person. Just ask Dick Sargent on Bewitched. That holds for an actor on Broadway just as it does for a baseball announcer arriving in a new city. Brian Anderson was named the television/cable play-by-play voice of the Brewers in 2007 and he's become an integral figure of the club's new winning identity. The organization thinks so much of Anderson they've extended his contract with a multi-year deal. The Milwaukee Brewers' popular TV play-by-play announcer, whose national reputation has grown considerably in recent seasons with his work calling MLB, NBA, NFL and NCAA Tournament games.

Anderson, a Texas native, began his career with the Minor League San Antonio Missions where he called more than one thousand games.

"When I left baseball and went into golf I thought I was done with baseball," Anderson reflected. "It's difficult to get into the Major Leagues when you have no Major League experience."

Undaunted, Anderson says he pushed his chips to the middle of the table when he learned the Brewers opening was 'all-in.' It's a dream job by anyone's standards and in many instances a broadcaster starts to think it's never going to happen.

"I made it past the first cut and felt I had a pretty good demo," Anderson says. "I knew I had a chance. It was the greatest day of my career when they told me I was in the top twenty and they brought the final four into Milwaukee and I was lucky enough to be one of them."

He comes by his knowledge first-hand with a

brother, Mike, who played with the Reds and is currently a pitching coach in the Rangers' Minor League system. Anderson is known to millions of golf fans due to his work on The Golf Channel, where he worked as a host for national events, as well as a sideline reporter for the San Antonio Spurs. His style is engaging, his energy level is high, and he clearly is passionate about his work on and off camera.

"I thought it'd be a big challenge to fans to grow accustomed to a new voice," says Anderson, who replaced Daron Sutton when he accepted a similar position with the Diamondbacks. Anderson says the hardest part about working in the minor league system was to create and retain interest in the game for local fans.

"In the minors we're always pitching who was going to be the next Major Leaguer and imploring fans to come out to the park to see 'him' now, before he hits the big-leagues," he added. While there weren't many difference on the field in Double A compared to the majors, Anderson says there were many differences behind the scenes. You had to think on your feet because there was nobody else to do it.

"I didn't have an engineer for the broadcasts," Anderson says. "If something went wrong, I had to fix it. I soldered head set wires while calling a game." It's that kind of experience that keeps Anderson humble, an understanding of those around him. "I respect and appreciate the hard work (the engineers) do to make each broadcast seem effortless," he says.

Most broadcasters can cite an individual who proved to be instrumental in their decision to go into broadcasting. Anderson says he admired the work of

Jack Buck and Ernie Harwell.

"Harwell never thought he was bigger than the game," he observed. "He once told me, 'MLB games were easier to call than the minors.' Now I know what he means."

He explained he lets the action on the field do most of the talking. He understands a broadcaster has to possess a good sense of his audience. "Nine innings can seem like a long time," Anderson quipped.

"And you need constant focus and concentration."

Longtime Brewers broadcaster Bill Schroeder has worked with a few play-by-play announcers in his career. Anderson feels honored to work with a pro.

"Bill is a great teacher," Anderson says. "My goal, with any partner, is to make sure the analyst is the star of the show. If the analyst shines, the sideline reporter shines; it makes my job easier and it makes me look great."

Anderson plays off Schroeder's commentary – a key to any good announcer's job. He says Schroeder can relate to so many situations because he played the game.

"We work so much together, we get a feeling for each other's strengths," he says. "I tee it up for him and he knocks it out of the park."

Milwaukee was uncharted territory for Anderson but admitted that the transition could not have gone better.

"The fans in Milwaukee have been really great to me," he added. "I was an unknown and I know they take their baseball very seriously. I never take my responsibility lightly."

"People talk to me as though they know me, as a friend," he says. "That's what's really interesting about this job and a little intimidating.

Baseball announcers walk a thin line between informing viewers and being too loquacious, overwhelming the audience with too much information they can see for themselves.

"I have a grading system on calls ranging from 1-10," Anderson says, "with 10 being the loudest." Anderson pointed out that a broadcaster doesn't want to peak too early in the season, like a home run call in April.

"If you do that," he says, "you don't have anything left when a home run puts you into the playoffs, you have to build and I do that with volume, tone and pitch. Bob Costas taught me that. The volume can dictate the sense of urgency."

As in chess, Anderson says he has to think three pitches or outs ahead. "Before every pitch I have to determine and evaluate what kind of moment it will be, 1-10," he says.

Fans of the film Spinal Tap will tell you— there's always room for eleven.

BILL SCHROEDER

It takes a lot of candor and humility for a former Major League ballplayer to give the lion's share of credit for his big league success to his parents.

In today's world of ludicrous salaries and 'what are you going to do for me' philosophy rampant in professional sports, it's truly refreshing to talk to an old-school type like Bill Schroeder.

Schroeder, a former Brewer and current color commentator on Milwaukee baseball broadcasts, looks like he could still lace them up with the legends of baseball. He was a hard-nosed player and earned the nickname *Rock.*

"I got that way back in AAA ball," Schroeder says. "There was a play at the plate in Vancouver. Kevin Bass, a former Brewers, threw the ball in. I took the mask off and it smashed me above the eye. Chuck Porter says it sounded like a rock hitting a wall. So that's where it came from."

"My mother and father were big influences in my career," Schroeder says. "They sacrificed quite a bit. My father would take me out for batting practice on Saturday morning instead of leaving me to watch cartoons."

If Schroeder was a Saturday morning cartoon character, he'd be Foghorn Leghorn—a big guy with a lot of heart and some rooster in him.

Schroeder spent eight years in the big leagues, first as a Brewer then as a California Angel, before the whole Anaheim thing.

Schroeder's father would take him to the local schoolyard in Princeton, New Jersey, and throw him baseballs over and over again. It's the kind of perseverance to a child's development that makes you yearn for a gentler era.

"These days people are more willing to give the kids money and send them to games," Schroeder says. ""They don't want to be in the trenches with the kids while they work on their batting swing. They don't want to donate their tie as a coach."

Schroeder says his parent's sense of duty and care was an essential part of his character development, giving him the security to become confident enough in his own skills to make it on a Major League level. The efforts by Schroeder's mother would make the schedule of today's soccer moms look like they're at Club Med.

"I'd have a game after school and then a Babe Ruth game after that. My mother would have a meal wrapped in aluminum foil and I'd be in the back seat eating my dinner while changing my uniform for the next game."

KENT SOMMERFELD

Kent Sommerfeld didn't wake up one morning and say, 'I want to work with the Brewers for 23 years and be an integral part of Bob Uecker's Hall-of-Fame broadcasting career.'

"There was no way I could have planned how it worked out," Sommerfeld, the producer on the Brewers Radio Network, recently says from his perch in the broadcast booth at Miller Park.

Sommerfeld was baptized into the big leagues with the nickname 'Sammy,' a seminal moment from the fertile and jocular mind of former Brewers broadcaster, and current Cubs announcer, Pat Hughes.

"Pat once says I look a little like Sammy Khalifa (former Pirates infielder) and Bob says I looked like (singer/actor) Sammy Davis, Jr.," Sommerfeld says in his quiet voice, accepting the moniker. "It stuck!"   A graduate of UW-Whitewater, Sommerfeld started his career broadcasting college basketball games at his alma mater, calling their success all the way up to a Division III title.

"We'd pile into a van and go to the next town to do a broadcast," he recalled.

On campus, Sommerfeld was the sports director at Cable TV-6, co-hosting a "Sports Chat" show on WSUW-Radio. He also latched on with ESPN's technical staff whenever the national sports cable giant televised events in the Midwest.

A student hoping to follow in Sommerfeld's footsteps had better learn to do everything by the book, be determined and avoid shortcuts. Sommerfeld had the presence of mind and foresight to make the necessary connections and develop relationships. He met Bill Haig, then director of broadcasting for the Brewers, and made an impression.

"Bill told me of an opening for a morning show producer," Sommerfeld says. "But I didn't want to get up at two in the morning every day."

Most young radio-heads would have jumped at virtually any opportunity. Sommerfeld wanted to work in sports and stuck to his guns. It was a career risk he was willing to take. Haig respected him for it and never forgot him because of it.

He took his first pro gig with KRBC-TV, the NBC affiliate in Abilene, TX as a sports/news photojournalist before returning to his home state at Haig's request to accept a position in the Brewers radio booth in 1986.

Following the 1990 baseball season, Sommerfeld jumped at another opportunity, this time producing and directing men's basketball games at Marquette University during the Brewers offseason. He later assumed the role as host of the team's pregame programming and moved behind the microphone for women's basketball play-by-play in 1999 when he became the director of the MU Basketball Radio Network.

Employed in broadcasting for as long as he has, Sommerfeld worked with the crudest of radio technology, including 8-track tapes, cassettes, and then progressed to CD's and digital audio.

"Technology, particularly computers, has changed the way we work," he says. "Some of the basic stuff is the same, the nuts and bolts. Computers have allowed me to monitor other games more closely and keep Bob and Jim (Powell) better informed."

Today, Sommerfeld produces and engineers every Brewers' broadcast, making sure the gear is in place. He connects the microphones, communicates with the engineers at WTMJ, giving Uecker and Powell scoring updates from other big league games and scripts for commercials.

"I take care of the business of the show so Jim and Bob can concentrate on the game," he says. "These guys don't have any inflated egos. They're very easy to work with. I'm just a small part of this team."

When Sommerfeld first arrived on the scene to work the broadcasts, Uecker had some fatherly advice.

"You'll work hard, we'll be on top of our game, but we'll have a lot of fun here too," he remembered.

They've held up their end of that impromptu bargain. There is no other way their relationship could have survived this long. That isn't to say there aren't some rigors associated with the job. Close quarters with other men for half of a year can be a trying experience.

"When you're with people 180 days in a year, you are like family," Sommerfeld related. "You have your ups and downs. You tend to know what each other will do before they do it."

He admitted the travel is hard and like the players, it's tough to be away from family, especially when children are young. "Now that they're older, they get to enjoy some of the perks," he says. "(They) come to the games and hang out in the clubhouse."

Working with celebrities like Uecker and Powell has been an educational experience, Sommerfeld says.

"You really get an idea of how big Uecker is when you're on the road," he added. "It's not really like that in Milwaukee. The people are used to him (here) and he can relax and be himself."

He's been doing this job so long that he's almost on auto-pilot. In 23 years Kent missed only four games, once for a wedding of a good friend, and a few days after getting injured in an accident.

"My job isn't any harder on the road as the equipment is basically the same," he says. "I have the same set up, my printer, my computers and audio boards. It's like a mini office both at home and on the road."

Bill Schroeder, the Brewers longtime broadcaster, knows Sommerfeld as well as anyone in the traveling party.

"Nobody gets more upset than Sammy when we're playing golf," Schroeder offered. "Nobody gets their chops busted more than Sammy, and he just takes it, smiles, and he has that little chuckle. But, I've never heard an unkind thing says about Kent."

CORY PROVUS

I defy you to take a seat next to Bob Uecker, a man with more than half a century in professional baseball, and hold your own as a play-by-play announcer.   Uecker probably has a vintage bottle in his wine cellar older than his new broadcasting partner. Working a game with Uecker is a task requiring talent and a ton of confidence. Cory Provus, an accomplished 35-year old from Highland Park, Illinois, answered the Brewers call for an announcer after longtime favorite Jim Powell left to take a job with the Atlanta Braves.

Provus cut his teeth behind the microphone handling the Chicago Cubs pre-and post-game shows along with some play-by-play duties. Going through the talent search procedure for the Brewers' opening was fairly easy compared to the daunting eventual meeting with Mr. Baseball.

"After the interview process was the sit-down with Bob," Provus says. "After ten minutes he toasted me and told me I was the guy. I think he knew he could work with me right away."

Provus earned his broadcasting stripes as the voice of the University of Alabama-Birmingham Blazers where he handled radio play-by-play for the UAB football, men's basketball and baseball.

With some pre-existing tentacles in the broadcasting world, Provus says he knew he wanted into the business when he was old enough to know what his cousin did for a living. Brad Sham has been the voice of the Dallas Cowboys since 1977 and Provus sought his familial counsel early on, but the talent and success are products of Provus alone.

"Brad always told me to be honest when calling the games," Provus says. "I was sending out tapes during my freshman year in college and he told me to figure things out on my own."

Provus says Shram was direct with his criticism, brutally honest. "When I was with Syracuse I had an expression when doing football games that the flow of play was from left to right on your radio dial," Provus recalled. "He told me 'leave that alone.' I took his advice and did just that."

Provus says you can't teach someone to be a good play-by-play announcer, it's something you have to experience and hone yourself.

"Learn what works for you and what doesn't," he says. " It takes some time. I've kind of learned through osmosis."

When working Cubs games with one-time Brewers announcer Pat Hughes, Provus says just because he was the color commentator he didn't feel the need to shine with the audience. "I wasn't going to overshoot my skis and become 'Johnny Baseball,'" Provus pointed out. "People would have seen right through that."

Working with a new team presents a host of new challenges – getting to know the players, the flow of the organization, the history of the team.

"I think I have a pretty good feel for things," he says at the halfway point of the season.

An overlooked and hidden nuance of broadcasting is the understanding of when to talk, and equally as important when to keep silent. "During a game, silence can at times be golden," he added.

"You're taught from day one in college to *not* leave gaps, but in radio I think the fans need to hear the vendors, pick up the ambiance."

Announcers, particularly when new to a town, can be hit with undue criticism and put under a baseball microscope by fans. Provus tried not to take in too much ancillary information. "I don't read message boards, chat rooms, it's just something I don't do," he admitted.

"I understand these outlets provide a vent for fans, but it isn't something I concern myself with."

Broadcasters are often called to task as to who they root for, on the air and in their personal lives. While Highland Park is only a Prince Fielder home run down the road, it may as well be light-years away.

"I want the Brewers to win," Provus says. "Since I come from Chicago, friends and fans think I'm going to root for the Cubs and some didn't buy my allegiance to the Brewers.

Provus quickly recognized Milwaukee as a great baseball town with great ownership.

"I've been swallowed up by the town and the wonderful baseball environment," he says. "It's been part of the fabric of the town since the 1950s."

In addition to the new town, a broadcaster has to know the team and coaches.

"Early on I asked Doug Melvin (Brewers general manager) what he'd learned about Ken Macha," he says. "Doug told me Macha is a guy that really thinks things through before he speaks or makes a decision."

That type of inside information goes a long way towards a broadcaster's understanding of the mechanics of a team.

What about his relationships with players?

"I try to preserve certain boundaries," Provus says. "I'm in the clubhouse every day. Players see me and I see them. I think it's important to be in the clubhouse."

Certainly, there's a chance players will disagree with something he says during a broadcast. "There is a chance they could do that," Provus responded. "But after seeing me in the clubhouse every day they understand I'm speaking from first-hand knowledge and not just my opinions."

In the spring, Provus knew the players only by the names on the backs of their jerseys but as the days and months followed, a sense of camaraderie was born.

"In Spring Training, if I saw Mike Cameron make a nice catch, I didn't call him 'Cammy.' It just didn't feel right," Provus says. "Now that I know him, it feels much more comfortable and real."

As for the players' work ethic, "I have so much respect at the time they put in," he added. No doubt, Provus is happy with his career decisions. Doing what he does at this level also makes someone else proud.

"My mom still has tears in her eyes," Provus says. "It doesn't matter if it's at Wrigley Field or here. She's had the opportunity to see her son live the dream. I can see the pride in her eyes."

Provus is currently the play-by-play announcer for the Minnesota Twins.

ROBB EDWARDS

It's not a particularly flattering comment when someone tells an announcer, "you have a face for radio." In the case of Robb Edwards, Miller Park's public address announcer, his movie star good looks make him an exception to the rule.

The rich voice is very familiar to anyone who has attended Brewers home games over the last 15 years. Edwards, who has served as the PA man at County Stadium and Miller Park with a near-perfect attendance record, has been in Milwaukee for decades.

"I think fans mostly remember me from my radio days and working in the community," Edwards say. "I used to do a lot of commercials on television and volunteered on channels 10 and 36."

Edwards, a Milwaukee radio personality since 1969, replaced the legendary Bob Betts, who served as the Brewers PA announcer for more than 1,700 games and 23 seasons before succumbing to an illness in November 1998. The Brewers dedicated the Bob Betts Press Box at Miller Park in 2001. Betts played an integral role in Edwards' early days in the business.

One thing endearing about baseball is the passing of the torch, transferring the love of the game from generation to generation. Edwards was born and raised in Chicago as a Cubs fan.

"My grandpa was a big Cubs fan and worked at Standard Oil," Edwards says. "We'd always go to Wrigley field for the home opener and it was almost always against the Cardinals."

This pre-dates Ernie Banks and Ron Santo. One would need a baseball encyclopedia to figure out who the Cubs' players were in those days.

"We had seats behind the first base dugout," he added. "One star of the day was Clyde McCullough and he gave me his catcher's mitt."

Over the years, Edwards says he may have unfortunately misplaced that piece of memorabilia. Edwards also discusses his admiration of Pat Piper, the Cubs public address announcer in that era.

"Prior would sit behind home plate with a megaphone," Edwards laughs. "Management wanted to move him upstairs but he refused."

Edwards' family eventually moved to Wisconsin where he later attended Pius High School.

"I was a relatively good athlete," he says. "I played sports; ran track in college."

Edwards was the public address announcer for Marquette University basketball and as a result he says he fell in love with college basketball.

He says he preps before each home series, making sure he doesn't commit the ultimate cardinal sin, mispronouncing a players name or the horrific omission of failing to introduce a player altogether.

"I try to find a game with the team who is coming into town," Edwards says. "I listen to the announcers and how they're pronouncing names. I will double and triple check with the team public relations people when they arrive."

He added that he'll also touch base with visiting broadcasters to see how they pronounce a name. But, that is only part of his preparation.

"We have a meeting an hour before each game," Edwards noted. "Aleta Mercer, (Brewers senior director-entertainment & marketing) runs a tight ship making sure everything is scripted out and everything is in order."

Keeping focused on the game is extremely

important and at times a challenge. The press box can offer its own share of diversions and provide an opportunity for a slip-up.

"I'm totally into the game and watch intently," Edwards says. "I have to be in the moment."

In 2008, Edwards suffered a heart attack and underwent bypass surgery, a minor setback in his professional life, an eye opener in his personal life.

"I don't take life for granted any more," Edwards says. "I was a typical guy and got occasional pains in my chest or arm. I dismissed them and felt I could shake it off."

It took a third party to prompt Edwards to act. "I made my morning journey to a local service station and the attendant told me I didn't look well," he added. "I called the hospital and told them I was coming in."

Since the surgery, Edwards walks around the concourse at Miller Park before games, a practice he takes very seriously. Fans often say hello as he strides by. "I have to keep movin'," he tells them with a smile. "They seem to understand that I need to finish my workout."

He says he loves working at Miller Park.

"It's night and day," Edwards began. "County Stadium was a glorious place in its day. In the old press box, we were isolated from the fans. There was a little porch in front of us called the loge, but other than that, we were very far from the fans and the ambiance of the crowd."

He was so adamant about being part of the crowd feel, he expressed his opinions during the final configurations of the ball park. "They had me come in and talk about the placement of the public address announcer," Edwards says. "The first option was in the director's room and that was too much like the old situation at County Stadium. Then they told me an option was the pressroom and I jumped at that offering."

Edwards is amazed at the knowledge of baseball fans in Milwaukee and that speaks to the value of the team in the city. "Radio stations talk a lot of baseball," he says. "It's an informed bunch, especially for the size of the city."

Moreover, the consistent sellouts have fed his enthusiasm for the job.

"I love what I do, and I love the crowd," Edwards says proudly. "It wouldn't make any sense to me to do anything else."

PHIL ROZEWICZ

Everybody participates in the career-counseling thing in high school, trying to decide whether you want to be a doctor, lawyer or accountant.

The odds are pretty high that the notion of working for a Major League Baseball club didn't come up in the conversation. There are jobs and careers you enter by happenstance, others by sheer determination and fascination.

Phil Rozewicz runs the visiting clubhouse at Miller Park. Prior to that, he spent one season as the Brewers home clubhouse manager and five seasons as the umpire's room attendant at County Stadium.

What headhunter is going to come up with a game plan like that?

"I used to come to games as a kid," Rozewicz says. "I dreamed of being a (Milwaukee Brewers) player."

And even though he played four seasons for his West Milwaukee High School baseball team, that Major League vision never materialized. Most kids will tell you they dreamed of being a batboy or a ball girl for a big league club. Rozewicz was no different, only he took matters a step further than most.

"I cut class to come to a game and through a mutual friend I was introduced to 'Big Jim' Ksicinski, the former visiting clubhouse manager for many years."

Ksicinski started the same way as Rozewicz. He grabbed a broom in the clubhouse a hundred years ago and never let go until the behemoth finally retired.

"I guess I was awestruck by the players as any kid would be when I started," admitted Rozewicz, now the father of two young daughters, who loves running marathons in his spare time. "Most of the players on visiting teams today know who I am and have developed some sort of comfort level with me."

His season begins in January in Arizona for spring training.

"I have to please a lot of people," Rozewicz says. His job includes communicating with the front office, game day operations and the grounds crew. "A team may say they're not taking batting practice the next day. I have to let people know so they can adjust their routines."

Rozewicz is put in a tough situation when rival teams arrive in Milwaukee.

"It's kind of funny. When the Reds, Astros, Pirates come to town, the fans get on their case," Rozewicz says. "It gets especially loud and crazy when the Cubs come to town, and these are the players I see most often during the season. The guys I know the best."

So, in a manner of speaking, Rozewicz fraternizes with the enemy on a regular basis. In fact, it's his job to be kind to players who work Brewers fans into a lather.

"I develop a kind of relationship with these particular players, as opposed to players I only see once in a while," he says.

Since Miller Park opened its luxurious doors, visiting players have come to see Milwaukee in a new light. "With the old clubhouse the guys used to hate to come to Milwaukee," Rozewicz says.

That it was. The visitor's clubhouse in County Stadium was pretty rough by anyone's standards. Not unlike a dressing room you'd find in a city park or old high school. Walking into today's clubhouse is similar to what you'd find in a suite at a posh hotel, replete with leather couches, flat screen televisions and personal computers.

"When we moved to Miller Park, it was like the old television show The Jefferson's," Rozewicz joked. "It was like we were 'Movin' On Up.'"

Make no mistake. This is a tough job and Rozewicz has been doing this longer than most folks stay at any place of business.

For a night game, Rozewicz gets to the park around 9:00 a.m.

"Sometimes," he says, "there are coaches waiting for me to unlock the doors."

After the game, duties keep Rozewicz and his staff busy until 1:00 a.m. Rozewicz starts his day making coffee for the players, laying out equipment and uniforms.

"These guys today get here so early they basically get three square meals," Rozewicz says. "I'll put out a lunch, a light spread after batting practice, then a full dinner spread (after the game)."

The players have so many food items to choose from, they rarely are wanting for anything. "Just about anything they like to eat we'll have," he added. "Clubs are nutrition conscious. Many teams will send out a daily menu they want for the road trip."

To help meet the demands of all the meals, Rozewicz says he'll utilize about four or five caterers in town.

"Generally, I don't get too many special requests," he says. "They have so many options it's like walking into a deli."

Rozewicz has six people working with him meeting the needs of teams. His assistant, Ben Wilkes, will attend to some of the higher profile players.

"Guys like Albert Pujols get used to certain things," Rozewicz pointed out. "Pujols likes a grilled ham and cheese with ketchup. Ben will make sure he gets it."

Last year was particularly rewarding for Rozewicz as the Brewers made their way into the postseason. He understands baseball is a business, like any other, with one exception.

"Before game time, the guys are like a bunch of kids getting ready for a game," Rozewicz added. "It doesn't matter (how much they make), they're still excited. He does have a particular souvenir he cherishes.

"I have a jersey signed by Hideo Nomo," Rozewicz says. "He wrote two full paragraphs in Japanese. I couldn't understand any of it, but visiting interpreters read the message on the uniform and were in tears." Apparently Nomo has a pretty good sense of humor. The man produces day-in and day-out, like any dedicated employee. The schedule creates rigors on family life and they sometimes take their toll, but he's devoted to his daughters, and his job.

"I've worked hard and developed a good reputation," Rozewicz says. "Gordon Ash says he's heard good things about my work during the winter meetings. I take pride in every single day. I want to be the best at what I do."

PATRICK ROGO

He's the keeper of the keys.

Patrick Rogo has been the warehouse supervisor for more than 25 seasons, little is delivered, distributed or stored at Miller Park without his knowledge. Rarely is he out of the loop when it comes to fulfilling the needs in the front office or the clubhouse.

If Rawlings delivers a load of baseballs to the South Dock, they'll come to him first before heading to the clubhouse. If a new section of sod for the playing field is shipped to Milwaukee, it doesn't get planted at the ballpark until he signs for it. When a consignment of bobbleheads arrives for an upcoming promotion date, he makes sure they jiggle their way to the right department. Heck, even this publication is delivered to Rogo's attention before ever seeing the light of game day.

Rogo inventories everything on the premises; from office supplies to even Bob Uecker's Harley – Davidson motorcycle back when the Brewers announcer used to tool around town.

His expertise, however, isn't limited to the stockroom.

Need a ride? Pat's the man. Like the night in September, 1992, when former Brewers owner Allan H. (Bud) Selig returned to Milwaukee from a trip. He wanted to catch Robin Yount's attempt at history.

Yount needed one hit to become the 17th player to reach 3,000. Rogo was dispatched to the airport to pick up the boss and his party, which included Selig's wife and then Rangers owner George W. Bush. Even the start of the momentous game was delayed until the envoy arrived. Selig had already written his own chapter in the baseball history books that very day when he was named chairman of the executive council for Major League Baseball making him the acting commissioner. Rogo knew about it well before Mrs. Selig did.

"I asked her how it felt to be the 'first lady' of baseball," Rogo says of his conversation en route to County Stadium. "She was stunned. She didn't know what I was talking about."

Oops! But the Commissioner of Baseball didn't seem to mind Pat broaching the topic. In fact, he seemed thankful that he had broken the ice about his appointment.

Since then, Rogo's been on a first name basis with Mr. Selig….uh, Bud. "Whenever he and I happened to be in the press box he'd grab whoever he was with and says, 'You've got to meet Pat,'" Rogo beamed. "That's a great feeling."

That's how things started for Rogo back in 1992. Hired as a jack-of-all trades, Pat learned the ins-and-outs of old County Stadium in a hurry.

If there were seats that needed repairing, concrete that needed patching or replacing, or other maladies associated with an aging facility, Rogo was, quite literally, Patty on the spot. He first interviewed for a maintenance position in an office tucked in the old bleachers armed with a mechanical aptitude.

"Most of the stuff I did with the Brewers (back then) I had never done before," he admitted.

And neither did any of the Brewers maintenance staff. Milwaukee County, the proprietor of the facility, had turned over power and upkeep directly to the team.

"I'm not sure the Brewers knew what they were getting into," Rogo says of the enormity of the job to run the ballpark. "I had worked in refrigerator repair and hadn't done anything in a ballpark.

But like everything else, he learned on the job.

"It's been an incredible place to work," Rogo reflected. "Sometimes I don't even look at it as a job."

Like the time he was asked to pinch-hit as a bat boy?

"I used to fill in for the kids when they went back to school in the fall," Rogo says. "I saw Sosa's 65th home run."

And, every time, or it seemed, Rogo worked as a bat boy, the Brewers won. One time, the Club was mired in a slump on the road and Pat got a call at home.

"When the team was on a seven game losing streak, then-Manager Phil Garner called me from Chicago," Rogo offered. "(He) told me to come down there to Wrigley Field and be the bat boy."

Part of Rogo's job, whether it's in his job description or not, is dealing directly with players. Now don't get too excited. He would help them with mailing packages or tracking packages, not necessarily with improving their swing.

"Rule number one from the first day I started working was never bother the players," Rogo says. "This is their sanctuary."

There is a strict policy among employees which clearly states don't ask players for autographs. "Generally, we shouldn't address them unless they talk to us first," he added. "They have a job to do and don't need to be distracted."

Though over time, Pat did foster a friendship with Hall of Famer Robin Yount.

"I've known Robin for a long time," Rogo began, "and I think one of the reasons he likes me is I've never asked him for anything."

He's seen his share of quirky things, too, most notably the floods, both at County Stadium and at Miller Park.

"Picture me standing on the dugout steps in County Stadium and the water was up to that," he says demonstrating the height being around four feet. "The flood in County Stadium was different as the field was much lower than the service areas. Most of the water back then was contained to the field."

Last year's Miller Park torrent, 'a monsoon' according to Rogo, did more monetary destruction. "We lost a lot," Rogo says.

From promotional items to archived material to perishables goods. "We even lost a lot of golf carts."

He was on hand when President Bush tossed out the first pitch at Miller Park. He actually watched the Commander-in-chief warm up just feet from his office. "He threw pretty well," Rogo recalled, "until they put the protective vest on him. That messed up his throwing arm."

Rogo contributed to the Brewers' successful On Deck event back in January. "They (the media relations department) asked me if there were any trophies they could display," he says of an area at the Midwest Center that featured a 40th anniversary theme.

"I told them we had the 1982 American League Championship trophy in the conference room (at Miller Park)."

Nobody knew what he was talking about despite the fact they'd walked by it hundreds of times. "It looks like a candy dish," Rogo chuckled. "Nobody could believe it was actually the trophy."

Rogo is also the curator of some valuable historical pieces tucked away in the warehouse use, including the old bullpen car in the shape of a baseball.

"Former Brewers executive Laurel Prieb was going to get rid of it but I think I convinced him it was something we should keep," Rogo says. "We've still got the original switchboard from County Stadium with all the cords to different extensions that Betty Grant used to handle."

Perhaps what endears Rogo most to the Brewers are his memories as a youngster going to the ballpark on sunny summer afternoons free of charge. Well, sort of.

"I used to sneak into County Stadium through a hole in the fence near the bleachers," Rogo jokingly confessed, confident the statute of limitations has long expired. "When I started doing maintenance, it (the hole) was still there. That was one of the first things I fixed."

"42"

There was something special going on at the Marcus Northshore Cinema; you could feel it.

The acclaimed movie "42," based on the life of baseball pioneer Jackie Robinson, was playing, but there was more happening. There was a unique and immediate connection with the film due to the presence of Jackie Robinson's daughter, Sharon. The audience of sixth-through eighth-grade students from roosevelt Middle School in Milwaukee seemed to feel it, too.

On April 15, 1947, the Brooklyn Dodgers started Robinson at first base, ending a racial segregation that had relegated black players to the Negro leagues.

While a milestone for baseball, this was a move that shook people to their core. An unthinkable move for some; a black man sharing the baseball field with white players.

After the screening of the film for about 50 students, Major League Baseball Commissioner Bud Selig stood onstage, alongside Sharon Robinson. Behind them on the screen was a huge still shot from the movie depicting Robinson trotting toward home plate, which gave an immediacy and perspective to the film and what Robinson and Selig had to say.

Sharon Robinson has worked for Selig and Major League Baseball for more than 16 years, developing the Breaking Barriers in Sports and Life organization.

"This is our first opportunity to share the film with students," Robinson says. "I particularly wanted to see their response to different parts of the film."

Robinson says the movie is all about breaking

barriers. She says everyone should be treated equally and believe in his or her abilities. One of the students asked Robinson about racism and how her father would deal with it today.

"He would say we've come a long way, but there's more to do," she says. "My father marched with Dr. Martin Luther King, wrote columns in newspapers and he'd always say, 'Don t' let them knock you down.'

Robinson has written numerous children's books and told the audience she didn't start writing until she was older.

"You should keep a journal," she told the kids. "You can write things in your journal you never tell anybody else; your own thoughts.

Robinson says "42" would allow children to have discussions about racism at home, not just accept it; "I think this movie will help them do that. Help them be prepared."

"You just saw in this film the most important and powerful moment in baseball history," Bud Selig told the audience.

Jackie Robinson was met with controversy and hatred at every turn when he came into the big leagues. This was 18 years before the civl rights movement, Selig says.

For Selig, recognition for Robinson seems to be a lifelong avocation. Under Selig's tenure as commissioner, each MLB team has retired uniform No. 42 in honor of Robinson, who wore that number while playing for the Dodgers.

In 2004, MLB began officially celebrating April 15 as Jackie Robinson Day, which features every player in every ballpark wearing Robinson's number.

Selig says he hoped new generations would l'd begin to understand what Robinson meant to the Civil

Rights Movement and equality of all people.

"He's one of the most important people of the 20th century," he says.

Jackie Robinson was familiar with a lot of firsts. He was the first black television analyst in MLB, and the first black vice president of a major American corporation.His life was chronicled in numerous television and stage venues. Young actor Chadwick Boseman took on the role of Robinson in "42," Blair Underwood played Robinson in "Soul of the Game," as did distinguished actor Andre Braugher in "The Court-Martial of Jackie Robinson."

Always the visionary, 10 days before his death, Robinson told Selig he would love to see a black manager in the dugout. After Robinson's death in 1972, Frank Robinson became the first black manager in 1975 with the Cleveland Indians.

Selig's love and respect for the Robinson family was evidenced when he politely asked interviewers if he could interrupt the session and say goodbye to Robinson, and hugged her.

"Without Robinson, we would never have seen Willie Mays, Henry Aaron play the game," he says. "That's part of why Jackie Robinson is important to me."

25527987R00079

Printed in Great Britain
by Amazon